'Dokumenty!'

Discrimination on grounds of race in the Russian Federation

Cover: An armed policeman checking identity documents in
Moscow, February 2000.
© Dmitry Lebedev/Kommersant

Amnesty International is a worldwide movement of people who campaign for internationally recognized human rights to be respected and protected.

Amnesty International's vision is of a world in which every person enjoys all of the human rights enshrined in the Universal Declaration of Human Rights and other international human rights standards.

In pursuit of this vision, Amnesty International's mission is to undertake research and action focused on preventing and ending grave abuses of the rights to physical and mental integrity, freedom of conscience and expression, and freedom from discrimination, within the context of its work to promote all human rights.

In this context it:

- seeks the release of prisoners of conscience: these are people detained for their political, religious or other conscientiously held beliefs or because of their ethnic origin, sex, colour, language, national or social origin, economic status, birth or other status – who have not used or advocated violence;
- works for fair and prompt trials for all political prisoners;
- opposes without reservation the death penalty, torture and other cruel, inhuman or degrading treatment or punishment;
- campaigns for an end to political killings and "disappearances";
- calls on governments to refrain from unlawful killings in armed conflict;
- calls on armed political groups to end abuses such as the detention of prisoners of conscience, hostage-taking, torture and unlawful killings;
- opposes abuses by non-state actors where the state has failed to fulfil its obligations to provide effective protection;
- campaigns for perpetrators of human rights abuses to be brought to justice;
- seeks to assist asylum-seekers who are at risk of being returned to a country where they might suffer serious abuses of their human rights;
- opposes certain grave abuses of economic, social and cultural rights.

Amnesty International also seeks to:

- cooperate with other non-governmental organizations, the United Nations and regional intergovernmental organizations;
- ensure control of international military, security and police relations, to prevent human rights abuses;
- organize human rights education and awareness raising programs.

Amnesty International is a democratic, self-governing movement with more than a million members and supporters in over 140 countries and territories. It is funded largely by its worldwide membership and public donations.

Amnesty International is independent of any government, political ideology, economic interest or religion. It does not support or oppose any government or political system, nor does it support or oppose the views of the victims whose rights it seeks to protect. It is concerned solely with the impartial protection of human rights.

'*Dokumenty!*'

Discrimination on grounds of race in the Russian Federation

Amnesty International Publications

Please note that readers may find some of the photographs and case histories contained in this report disturbing.

First published in 2003 by
Amnesty International Publications
International Secretariat
Benenson House
1 Easton Street
London WC1X 0DW
United Kingdom

http://www.amnesty.org/russia

Printed by:
The Alden Press
Osney Mead
Oxford
United Kingdom

CONTENTS

GLOSSARY

CIS	Commonwealth of Independent States
CERD	Committee on the Elimination of Racial Discrimination
CPT	European Committee for the Prevention of Torture and Inhuman or Degrading Treatment or Punishment
State *Duma*	Lower House of Parliament
ECRI	European Commission against Racism and Intolerance
FMS	Federal Migration Service
FSB	Federal Security Service
GUVD	Main Department of Internal Affairs
ICCPR	International Covenant on Civil and Political Rights
ICESCR	International Covenant on Economic, Social and Cultural Rights
MVD	Ministry of the Interior
OSCE	Organization for Security and Co-operation in Europe
OVIR	Department for Visas and Registration
NGO	Non-governmental organization
RUBOP	Regional Organized Crime Squad, a law enforcement agency
UNHCR	United Nations High Commissioner for Refugees

The Russian Federation and surrounding countries

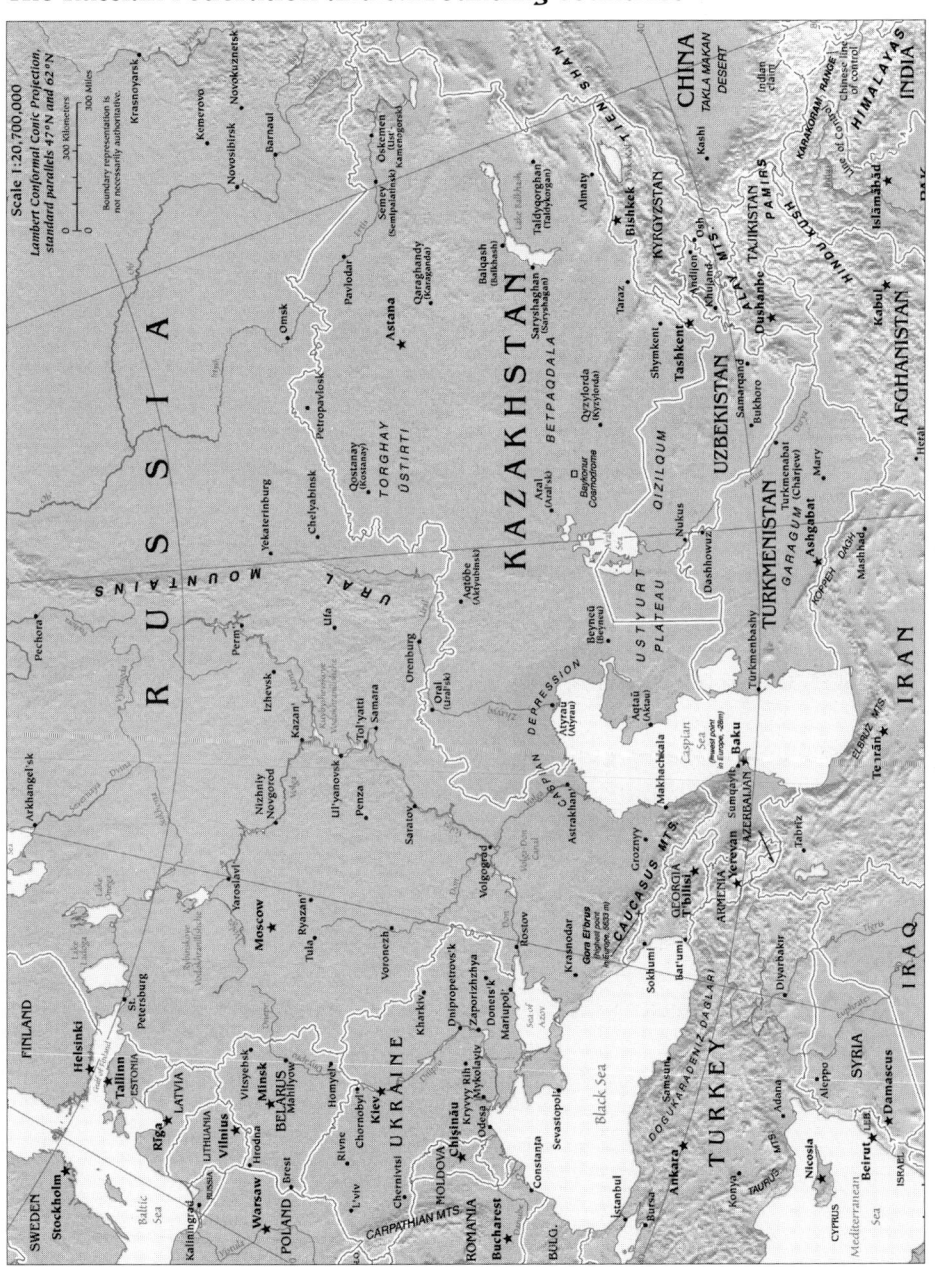

© Courtesy of The General Libraries, The University of Texas at Austin, USA

Bondepadhai Suif (*right*), a medical student from India, was one of three Asian students reportedly attacked by skinheads on 10 March 2002 in Ivanovo, near Moscow. All three were hospitalized and one, a student from Bangladesh, later died after spending several weeks in a coma. In this instance, according to reports, the police did respond and a criminal investigation was started which resulted in several arrests. All too often, however, racist violence is neither investigated nor punished.

Chapter 1: Introduction

"Putin has said that everyone should feel at home here, and that is of course welcome. But we want to feel safe, not at home."

Petrus Indongo, General Secretary of the Association of African Students at the Russian University of Peoples' Friendship, Moscow

A summer picnic in Troparevskii Park, Moscow, should have provided the participants with a few hours' escape from everyday cares. Instead, African students, refugees and asylum-seekers taking part were brutally attacked by a group of about 10 Russian men with shaven heads shouting racist abuse.

The attack took place as the picnickers were leaving the park at 8pm on 13 July 2002. They asked traffic police stationed nearby to call for help and approached a police officer sitting in his car; he told them to go away. They stopped a passing police car, but the officers in it said that the area was outside their jurisdiction and refused to help.

The police finally arrived half an hour later. By this time all but two of the alleged attackers had left and their victims had been joined by the Reverend John Calhoun and his wife, Dr Noel Calhoun, who had organized the picnic, as well as women and children who had also been at the picnic.

One of the officers, a criminal investigation officer, immediately accused the picnickers of starting the fight because "there are 20 of you and only two Russians". When eyewitnesses to the attack tried to tell him what they had seen, the officer ignored them. Instead, he started questioning the picnickers about their identities and status: "Where are you from? Are you legally in Moscow? What is the legal address of your church? Where is it registered? Are you all legally registered? Are you Africans or African-Americans?" Dr Calhoun asked the officer for his full name, but he refused to answer. Other officers checked the identity documents of those present.

Some of the picnickers who had documents issued by the United Nations High Commissioner for Refugees (UNHCR) had already left. Police generally do not recognize these documents as valid forms of identification. Refugees and asylum-seekers, therefore, generally avoid contact with the police as such contact often results in their being arbitrarily detained or fined (see Chapter 8).

One of the picnickers, Germain Soumele Kembou, a student from Cameroon, suffered serious injuries during the attack. Despite needing hospital treatment, he was taken to the police station at Teplyi Stan with the two alleged attackers for questioning.

A witness described to Amnesty International how when Germain Soumele Kembou arrived at the police station, three young men matching the description given of the attackers were waiting on the front steps. One of them shouted "White Power" in full view of Germain Soumele Kembou and the police.

As Germain Soumele Kembou's condition was deteriorating and there was no sign of an ambulance, the Reverend and Dr Calhoun insisted on taking him for emergency treatment. After being stopped for questioning by police on the way, they finally arrived at Yasenovo accident and emergency unit at 10.30pm. Several police officers then arrived and tried to insist that Germain Soumele Kembou return to the station immediately. He was finally admitted to hospital only after a Cameroonian embassy representative intervened. Germain Soumele Kembou reached Botkin Hospital at 2am, several hours after the attack.

This case is unusual in that it received considerable media attention and a criminal investigation was opened. Several refugees were willing, with the help of UNHCR lawyers, to put their complaints in writing, including complaints about police failure to provide them with protection. However, the most unusual aspect of the case is that the charge[1] refers to "aggravating circumstances", acknowledging the racist nature of the attack.[2]

The investigation was continuing at the time of writing.

Discrimination on grounds of race is a reality for many members of ethnic or national minority groups in the Russian Federation. Victims whose cases have come to the attention of Amnesty International are predominantly students, asylum-seekers and refugees from Africa, but also include citizens of the Russian Federation (including ethnic Chechens and Jews), as well as people from the south Caucasus, from South, Southeast and Central Asia, from the Middle East and from Latin America.

Amnesty International's research shows how legislation governing registration and citizenship requirements is often applied in a discriminatory way by agents of the state. In some cases, particular groups are targeted disproportionately by police for checks of their identity documents, often leading to arbitrary detention or ill-treatment (see chapter 6). Asylum-seekers and refugees suffer the additional difficulty that their documentation is not recognized by the police (see chapter 8). In some regions the legislation in practice denies whole communities their right to a range of economic, civil and political rights, including their right to citizenship (see chapter 7).

As in many other countries, law enforcement agencies in the Russian Federation often reflect rather than challenge discriminatory attitudes in society at large. Amnesty International's research indicates that many racist attacks are not reported to the police because the victims fear further abuses by the police themselves. Racist attacks are often dismissed as the actions of drunken teenagers which the police then fail to register as racially motivated or to investigate. The result is that victims of racist crime rarely see justice done, that police and members of the public feel that racism is tolerated, and that members of ethnic minorities feel that they have no one to turn to.

Racism is an attack on the very notion of universal human rights. It systematically denies certain people their full human rights because of their colour, race, ethnicity, descent or national origin. The right to be free from racial discrimination is a fundamental principle of human rights law. Under international human rights law, governments are obliged to combat discrimination in all its forms. They have a responsibility to ensure that laws and institutions of the state address the root causes and consequences of discrimination.

Yet racial discrimination persists in virtually every society, despite all the efforts of the UN and organizations around the world dedicated to combating racism, and the fine-sounding commitments in so many constitutions and laws.

Whether inflicted by agents of the state or by private individuals or groups in the community at large (non-state actors), racism is intimately linked to the subordinate or marginalized position which those targeted for discrimination hold in society. The failure to hold to account those who commit, encourage or acquiesce in racist abuse frequently exacerbates the problem and helps create a climate of impunity for those who commit such acts.

> The Russian Federation is a state party to the International Convention on the Elimination of All Forms of Racial Discrimination. The Convention obliges the authorities to take active measures to prohibit and eliminate discrimination on grounds of race, colour, descent, or national or ethnic origin and to guarantee to everyone equality before the law.

This report, which was written in September 2002, is not intended to be a comprehensive survey of all the national, ethnic or racial groups in the Russian Federation who are subjected to discrimination. It highlights particular groups who have been the subject of Amnesty International's research. There are numerous other groups, cases and issues that could have been included. The fact that the report focuses on particular groups does not imply that these are the sole or principal victims of racial discrimination, or that the experiences suffered by other victims are of less concern. Nor should the highlighting of a particular manifestation of discrimination disguise the fact that different forms of discrimination are interlinked. The identity of every human being is complex and cannot be reduced to one sole factor such as race, ethnicity, gender, sexual orientation or class.

People with the power and responsibility to initiate change are now acknowledging that racism is a serious problem in the Russian Federation. For example, President Vladimir Putin and the Prosecutor General have made public statements that racist offences will not be tolerated and that those responsible will be treated with "the maximum strictness allowed by law."[3] President Putin has also made statements recognizing that Russian citizens from Chechnya have been unfairly identified with "terrorism" and other criminal activities.

These statements stand in stark contrast to practices in the past, and which persist in certain regions of the Russian Federation, of influential people inflaming prejudices against members of ethnic minorities for reasons of political expediency. The parliamentary and presidential elections in December 2003 and March 2004 will test whether the Russian Federation can avoid the tendency seen in many other countries to scapegoat ethnic minorities for political gain.

Positive measures against racism are being initiated. In 2001 the authorities initiated a five-year State Program on Tolerance and Prevention of Extremism in Russian Society, which envisages a wide-ranging program of reforms under the auspices of the Ministry of Education. The Program aims to change attitudes and practices which facilitate discrimination on grounds of race and religion. The introduction of the office of human rights ombudsman in all the regions of the Russian Federation will offer another potential mechanism for change. Legislation is being updated and ministries are being called upon, for example, to devise effective and comprehensive policies on immigration and migration.

Non-governmental organizations (NGOs) in the Russian Federation, who joined forces during the 2001 UN World Conference against Racism, Racial Discrimination, Xenophobia and Related Intolerance[4] to highlight their concerns, have continued to do substantial work in monitoring racial discrimination, fighting racism through the courts, supporting individual victims of racism and lobbying for change.

The Council of Europe, the European Union (EU), the Organization for Security and Co-operation in Europe (OSCE) and the UN have all raised their concerns about racism and discrimination in the Russian Federation and have made recommendations to the authorities. The government will have to show greater commitment to respect international standards and to implement such recommendations if it is to ensure that people's fundamental rights are respected.

This report ends with a series of Amnesty International's own recommendations to combat racism in the Russian Federation. These recommendations, and indeed the report as a whole, are intended to support and contribute to the ongoing work of individuals and organizations working both within the Russian Federation and as part of the international human rights movement to ensure that the right to be free from racial discrimination becomes a reality for all.

This report is being published as part of Amnesty International's major worldwide campaign against human rights abuses in the Russian Federation. The campaign seeks to highlight the discrepancy between the human rights protection which those

living in the Russian Federation have in international and national law, and the reality of widespread human rights abuses committed by agents of the state and non-state actors in a climate of impunity. Amnesty International members around the world are urging the government to live up to its obligations to protect, respect, ensure and promote human rights so that there is *justice for everybody*.

A group of international students in Moscow protesting against racism.

Amnesty International's work against racism

Amnesty International opposes racism through its work to promote observance around the world of the range of rights enshrined in the Universal Declaration of Human Rights. It calls for ratification and implementation by states of international and regional human rights instruments that prohibit all forms of discrimination. It also works worldwide on cases of grave violations of the right to be free from discrimination, including racial discrimination.

Amnesty International's work to combat racism includes campaigning for the release of prisoners of conscience[5] imprisoned solely on account of race, descent, or national or ethnic origin; and working on cases where racism is a factor in abuses including torture, ill-treatment, the death penalty, "disappearances", unfair trials of political prisoners,[6] unlawful killings, excessive use of force, forcible exile, mass expulsions and house destruction. The organization also opposes discriminatory legislation that facilitates these violations. In addition, Amnesty International intervenes when racial discrimination prevents redress for victims and perpetuates impunity for perpetrators of human rights abuses, or hinders the right of those fleeing persecution to seek asylum.

Amnesty International's work against discrimination on the grounds of race, descent, colour, ethnicity or national origin is based on the definition set out in Article 1(1) of the International Convention on the Elimination of All Forms of Racial Discrimination:

"In this Convention, the term 'racial discrimination' shall mean any distinction, exclusion, restriction or preference based on race, colour, descent, or national or ethnic origin which has the purpose or effect of nullifying or impairing the recognition, enjoyment or exercise, on an equal footing, of human rights and fundamental freedoms in the political, economic, social, cultural or any other field of public life."

In 2001 Amnesty International published *Racism and the administration of justice*[7] as part of its contribution to the struggle against racism and specifically to the debate centred on the 2001 UN World Conference against Racism.[8]

An Armenian grave vandalized by skinheads, Krasnodar city, Krasnodar Territory, April 2002.

"In the beginning we didn't even consider it 'abroad'. It was a big surprise to realize that people saw us as 'foreigners'...

We had studied Russian literature, Russian music...

Since [Governor] Tkachev's speech in March officials have seen that they can treat us like dirt. But Tkachev claims there is no link between what he says and what happens...

People said [the attack on the cemetery] was just bandits and other graves were attacked too. It's not true...

It is funny. Every Russian says, 'We like you. It is the others we don't like.' No doubt each Armenian knows someone like that."

Karina, an Armenian woman living in Krasnodar, May 2002.

Chapter 2: Ethnicity and nationality in the Russian Federation

The population of the Russian Federation is composed of a wide variety of ethnic groups. Although around 84 per cent of the population is made up of ethnic Russians, some 100 other distinct ethnic or national groups are also represented.

The Russian Federation emerged as a sovereign state in 1991 from the collapsing Soviet Union which had in 1917 inherited the rich diversity of peoples and cultures of the former territory of the Tsarist empire. This empire had fought for hundreds of years to extend and consolidate its boundaries, often using as its front line semi-military Slav communities, known as Cossacks, who in return received certain privileges. By the second half of the 19th century the Tsarist empire had achieved control over the peoples of the Caucasus and Central Asia.

Soviet nationality policy was applied in different ways in different periods. In the years immediately following the 1917 revolution, which saw the birth of the Soviet Union, the emphasis was on the cultural autonomy of minorities, although a political tactic of "divide and rule" could also be discerned. Under Commissar for Nationalities Joseph Stalin, the right to self-determination receded, reinforced by widespread arrests of political and cultural leaders throughout the Soviet Union. During the Second World War the leaders of the Soviet Union initiated wholesale forcible removal of peoples they perceived as potential enemies within, on the sole basis of their ethnic or national origin, or as politically "inconvenient" on the basis of their location. Among those forcibly relocated to other territories within the Soviet Union were Chechens, Ingush, Karachais, Balkars, Meskhetians, Crimean Tatars, Pontic Greeks, Kurds, Koreans, Kalmyks, and Germans from the Volga and Ukraine.

Until Stalin's death in 1953, banished people were subject to severe restrictions on their movements which required them to sign on at police stations weekly and imposed severe penalties for any movement outside the area where they were registered.

© ITAR-TASS

In October 2001 a crowd of between 150 and 300 youths brandishing iron bars attacked Tsaritsyno market in Moscow, which is largely staffed by ethnic minorities. Three men – an ethnic Armenian, an Indian and an ethnic Tajik – were killed in the attacks, and about 30 people were hospitalized. Initial police reports referred to the perpetrators as "football hooligans". Five young men were charged with involvement in the attack.

Although such restrictions were lifted after 1953, practical realization of the right to return to their original homes was for many impossible and public discussion of the forcible relocations was suppressed.

Anti-semitism was often official policy in the former Soviet Union, both under Stalin and after his death in 1953. This was usually masked under the rubric of "anti-Zionism" and often used modified versions of the crude imagery of Tsarist Russia or indeed Nazi Germany.[9]

During the 1970s and 1980s many people adopted as prisoners of conscience by Amnesty International had been imprisoned or internally exiled for their opposition to what they saw as an official policy of "Russification", which prevented them using their own language as a public medium, or celebrating their own national cultural figures.

In 1989, in the period of liberalization known as *perestroika*, the government of the Soviet Union issued a declaration on the "Savage acts carried out by the Stalinist regime" in deporting and imprisoning various peoples. Commissions were set up to resolve practical problems associated with restoring their rights.[10] However, the rehabilitation process for certain peoples, such as the Meskhetians, was interrupted when the Soviet Union ceased to exist in 1991. Many other issues, such as the right to return to one's home, the right to have a Russian passport and the right to compensation, have also remained unresolved to this day.

The 1989 census of the former Soviet Union identified 113 ethnic communities, or "nationalities", having populations of 1,000 or more, as well as several dozen groups numbering in the hundreds.[11] Almost all had their own languages, customs and religious traditions. Fifteen nationalities (Russian, Ukrainian, Uzbek, Belarusian, Kazak, Azeri, Armenian, Tajik, Georgian, Moldavian, Lithuanian, Turkmen, Kyrgyz, Latvian, and Estonian) were accorded separate republics within the Soviet Union. Several dozen other groups were assigned autonomous regions or territories. All were citizens of the one entity, the Soviet Union.

The end of the Soviet Union saw these republics emerge as 15 sovereign states, the largest of which is the Russian Federation. Each contained ethnic or national minorities. All citizens of the former Soviet Union had the same passport, indicating the person's place of birth and their "nationality"[12] but denoted only one citizenship — that of the Soviet Union. These passports have remained in use, only gradually being replaced by passports of the new states or annotated to denote citizenship of a particular republic. However, in December 2003 the old passports will cease to be legally valid, possibly leaving millions of people, for various reasons, stateless.

The break-up of the Soviet Union was accompanied by several conflicts, both within the Russian Federation — where the most long lasting is that taking place in Chechnya — and beyond its borders, for example, in Tajikistan where hundreds of thousands of people were displaced by the fighting in the early 1990s.

A girl in Ingushetia stands at the entrance to a former chicken farm used to house people fleeing the fighting in Chechnya.

Chechnya has suffered more than six years of armed conflict characterized by widespread human rights abuses. More than 300,000 people have been displaced by the fighting; many have fled to neighbouring Ingushetia.

The Russian authorities signed a repatriation plan in May 2002. Amnesty International has received credible reports that displaced Chechens in the tent camps of Ingushetia have been put under intense pressure to return home.

In other parts of the Russian Federation, Chechens displaced by the conflict are often refused forced migrant status and are thus unable to receive humanitarian aid from the state.

Amnesty International has urged the authorities to ensure that all people internally displaced by the conflict are given adequate protection and humanitarian assistance until they can return voluntarily, in safety and with dignity, to their place of origin or choice. The current situation in Chechnya does not provide the necessary conditions for the safe and durable return of internally displaced people. There are continuing reports of attacks against civilians, rape and other forms of torture, "disappearances", and extrajudicial executions by Russian forces.

The first conflict in Chechnya (1994 to 1996) ended with a peace settlement which resulted in the withdrawal of Russian federal troops. However, in September 1999, Russian federal troops were once again sent to Chechnya. The ensuing conflict has been characterized by widespread human rights violations by the Russian forces. Chechen fighters have also reportedly committed human rights abuses. Although this report does not address the issue of human rights abuses within Chechnya, Amnesty International has documented cases of rape and other forms of torture, "disappearances", extrajudicial executions and direct attacks on civilians in several reports published in recent years.[13] The Russian authorities claimed that the triggers for sending troops into Chechnya in 1999 were a series of bombings of apartment buildings in Moscow and two other cities which killed hundreds of people and which the Russian authorities blamed on "Chechens", and an attack on several towns and villages in neighbouring Dagestan by up to 1,000 Chechen fighters.

The economies of many of the sovereign states which emerged from the Soviet Union remain weak and the more prosperous parts of the Russian Federation continue to attract migrant workers and small traders from most of the former Soviet republics, including Tajikistan, Azerbaijan, Ukraine, Moldova and Belarus.

The legacy of the former Soviet Union's policies towards the developing world can be seen in Moscow's importance as an international hub handling flights to and from dozens of countries in Africa, Asia and the Middle East. It is also reflected in the large number of students from Africa, in particular, who choose to study in the higher education institutions in the country: an estimated 1,000 African students are currently following courses at The Russian University of People's Friendship in Moscow, where staff and students represent 450 ethnicities from more than 100 countries.[14]

A society with such a complex and diverse heritage requires careful and considered statements by political leaders who demonstrate both in word and action their principled commitment to tolerance and respect for difference. Instead, the authorities have all too often used overtly discriminatory rhetoric for political advantage and to justify blatant violations of human rights.

While national and international law promises those living in the Russian Federation equality and protection from discrimination, procedures and practices on the ground, as well as local laws, mean that racial discrimination frequently goes unrecorded and unpunished. Indeed, the very authorities and institutions charged with upholding human rights are frequently complicit in such abuses.

The voices of those in the Russian Federation who seek to increase racial divisions and hostility in society have become increasingly strident. Amnesty International calls on the authorities to send a clear message, backing up words with deeds, that they will take the necessary measures to fulfil their obligation to promote and protect the right of all people to be free from discrimination.

Chapter 3: International standards

Usam Vakhaevich Baisaev of the Memorial Human Rights Center flew to Moscow from Ingushetia on 24 March 2001. He had been invited by Amnesty International to participate in its delegation attending the 57th session of the UN Commission on Human Rights and was due to fly on to Switzerland the following day.

He arranged to meet his aunt, Zainap Baisaeva, and to spend the night at her home in Moscow. As he was greeting his aunt, a police car stopped in the street beside them and two officers got out.

The officers asked Usam Baisaev for his papers. He showed them his identity documents, including his passport with Swiss visa, his identification card as assistant to a deputy of the state *Duma*, and his air ticket from Ingushetia. He told the officers that he had just arrived in the capital and was leaving for Switzerland the next day.

Usam Baisaev told Amnesty International that one of the officers seemed quite satisfied with his explanation, but the other officer began insulting him, saying that he hadn't spent time in Chechnya killing Chechens for nothing. "I wasn't killing Chechens there just so they could travel abroad". Then he threatened to have Usam Baisaev detained for at least a week.

Usam Baisaev was told that he would have to go to the local police station for verification of identity. When he asked the reasons for his detention, as his documents were in order, Usam Baisaev says the only answer the officer gave was that he was a Chechen.

Usam Baisaev's complaint to the Minister of the Interior of Ingushetia states:

"I haven't got a watch, so I didn't know how long we were driven around the city...

The lieutenant told me they could, as he said, 'put you for a long time in the doss-house' [15] *despite the documents I had shown them. He stressed the fact that the only punishment they would get for this would be a 'Well done, guys!' from their bosses.*

Then he asked if I had money. I told him that a man who is going abroad has to have some money. He proposed that I give him 500 rubles [approximately US$16] to solve the problem 'amicably'. I told him it was too much, but the officers refused to 'lower the price' of our freedom. They agreed to bring us back to where they had found us...

I also found out later that the officers had forced my aunt to pay up too. She didn't know I had already paid the 'ransom'." [16]

In April 2001 *Duma* Deputy Sergei Kovalev wrote to the Minister of the Interior of the Russian Federation raising this case. Later that month he was informed that the matter had been passed to Ziuzinskaia Inter-district Prosecutor's Office for examination. At the end of May, Zainap Baisaeva was questioned about the case by officials from that Office. No further progress was known to have been made at the time of writing.

The right to enjoy human rights without discrimination is a fundamental principle underlying international human rights law. The prohibition on discrimination is a fundamental part of the UN Charter and the Universal Declaration of Human Rights. The Russian Federation is party to several human rights treaties of particular relevance to race-related discrimination. These include the International Covenant on Civil and Political Rights (ICCPR), the International Covenant on Economic, Social and Cultural Rights (ICESCR), the Convention against Torture and Other Cruel, Inhuman or Degrading Treatment or Punishment, and the Convention on the Elimination of All Forms of Discrimination against Women. The Russian Federation has submitted reports on its implementation of the ICCPR and the ICESCR to the relevant treaty-monitoring bodies, the Human Rights Committee and the Committee on Economic Social and Cultural Rights respectively, which are scheduled to consider them in 2003. It is also a party to the principal UN treaty aimed at eliminating and prohibiting such discrimination, the International Convention on the Elimination of All Forms of Racial Discrimination.

© UCSJ

On 27 May 2002 Tatiana Sapunova noticed this anti-semitic placard at the side of the road while driving in the Moscow region. According to press reports, she stopped her vehicle and tried to pull the placard out of the ground. The placard was connected to an explosive device which went off, causing Tatiana Sapunova burns and facial injuries.

Days after the incident, a Moscow police chief reportedly told a national newspaper that he did not consider the slogan on the placard, which read "Death to Jews!", to be explicitly anti-semitic or an incitement to ethnic hatred.

Tatiana Sapunova was later awarded the Order of Courage by President Putin.

International Convention on the Elimination of All Forms of Racial Discrimination

The International Convention on the Elimination of All Forms of Racial Discrimination was adopted by the UN General Assembly in December 1965 and entered into force in January 1969. States which are party to this Convention have committed themselves to prohibit and eliminate racial discrimination by all appropriate means and to guarantee the right of everyone, without distinction as to race, colour, descent or national or ethnic origin, to equality before the law and to the enjoyment or exercise of their civil, political, economic, social and cultural rights on an equal footing.

The Convention obliges states not only to end discrimination by government officials, but to protect people from and prohibit racial discrimination and violence by private individuals, groups or organizations.[17]

The body established by the Convention charged with monitoring states' implementation of their obligations under the Convention is the Committee on the Elimination of Racial Discrimination (CERD). The CERD examines periodic reports submitted by states parties and issues conclusions and recommendations aimed at enhancing the state's implementation of the Convention. It also considers complaints from individuals or groups who claim that their rights under the Convention have been violated by a state party to the Convention, provided that state has recognized the competence of the CERD to do so and that remedies available within the state have been exhausted.[18]

In 1992 the government of the Russian Federation declared that it would continue to "perform the rights and to fulfil the obligations following from the international agreements signed by the USSR".[19] These agreements included several international human rights treaties ratified by the former Soviet Union, among them the International Convention on the Elimination of All Forms of Racial Discrimination. The Russian Federation has also recognized the competence of the CERD to consider complaints from individuals or groups claiming to be victims of violations of any of the rights set out in the Convention.[20]

Periodic reports submitted to the CERD

In 1995 the Russian Federation submitted its first reports to the CERD. These reports had been due in 1992 and 1994. This combined 12th and 13th periodic report[21] was considered by CERD in February 1996. The concerns expressed by the CERD[22] included failures of implementation of the principles and provisions of the Convention (particularly at regional and local

The International Convention on the Elimination of All Forms of Racial Discrimination requires governments to tackle racism in all its forms, including incitement to racial hatred. Article 282 of the new Criminal Code, which entered into force in January 1997, makes it a criminal offence to engage in deliberate acts intended to stir up national, racial or religious hatred or discord. In its 2002 report to the CERD, the government gave statistics for prosecutions under Article 282 since 1997:

- 1997 – 12 prosecutions;
- 1998 – 16 prosecutions.

In 1999 the Prosecutor's Office handled 44 cases under Article 282, of which only nine went to court; 18 cases were closed for various reasons and three were halted because the police failed to find the perpetrators.

It is clear from the government's own statistics that prosecutions are rarely initiated under this legislation and are almost never successful.

levels) and an increase in racist attitudes — and in particular anti-Chechen sentiments — among nationalist groups, local authorities and the general population, and indications of anti-semitism among part of the population.

The CERD recommendations included calling on the government to: carry out the decision of the Constitutional Court to abolish the registration permit system effectively; to provide the Committee with information on the number of complaints and court cases related to racial discrimination and their outcomes; and to train judges, lawyers, magistrates, law enforcement personnel and the military in human rights, in line with the CERD's General Recommendation XIII.[23]

In 1998, after considering the Russian Federation's 14th periodic report,[24] which was also submitted late, the CERD's Concluding Observations[25] welcomed provisions contained in the new Criminal Code that had entered into force on 1 January 1997.[26] However, the CERD expressed concern about the increasing incidence of acts of racial discrimination and inter-ethnic conflicts and the situation in Chechnya. It stated that it had received only limited information about efforts to investigate and punish acts of racial discrimination and to provide reparation. It repeated its call for domestic legislation to be fully implemented in order to guarantee in practice real enjoyment by all of the right to freedom of movement and residence and the right to a nationality. It reiterated its recommendations that training for judges and law enforcement officials in the protection of the rights of racial minorities continue and be developed.

The CERD was also concerned at serious human rights violations in Chechnya and called for the perpetrators of such violations to be punished and the victims to receive reparation. It urged that those displaced by the conflict be ensured "normal conditions of life".

In April 2002 the Russian Federation submitted a combined report to the CERD covering the period from January 1997 to February 2002.[27] This responds to previous CERD comments and highlights promotional and preventive initiatives taken in response. The report was scheduled to be considered by the CERD in early 2003.

Regional human rights standards

The Russian Federation is a party to the European Convention for the Protection of Human Rights and Fundamental Freedoms (European Convention on Human Rights). Article 14 states that the enjoyment of rights guaranteed by the Convention must be secured "without discrimination on any ground such as sex, race, colour, language, religion, political or other opinion, national or social origin, association with a national minority, property, birth or other status." Article 3 prohibits torture and other inhuman or degrading treatment. The European Commission of Human Rights held that race discrimination may itself constitute degrading treatment under this Article.[28]

In November 2000 the Council of Europe adopted a new treaty – Protocol No. 12 to the European Convention on Human Rights. This treaty prohibits discrimination by any public authority on grounds including sex, race, colour, language, religion, political or other opinion, national or social origin, association with a national minority, property, birth or other status. Protocol No. 12 thus extends the protection against discrimination enshrined in Article 14 of the European Convention on Human Rights, which applies only to the rights set out in the European Convention. This means that individuals in states which are parties to Protocol No. 12 should be protected from discrimination with regard to all of their rights, including those set out in national law and in other Council of Europe standards.[29]

The Russian Federation has signed but not yet ratified Protocol No. 12; as a signatory it is obliged not to take any action which contradicts the object and purpose of the treaty. Amnesty International continues to call on the Russian Federation to ratify this treaty.[30]

The Russian Federation is a party to the Council of Europe's Framework Convention for the Protection of National Minorities, which aims to protect national minorities within the territories of the states parties and to promote their full and effective equality. The treaty prohibits discrimination against national minorities and sets out the right of national minorities to equality before the law and equal protection. It requires states to take measures to protect people who may be subject to threats, acts of discrimination, violence or hostility as a result of their ethnic, cultural, linguistic or religious identity.

The Russian Federation is also a party to the European Convention for the Prevention of Torture and Inhuman or Degrading Treatment or Punishment. The Convention establishes and mandates a committee to undertake unrestricted on-site visits to any place where individuals are deprived of their liberty by a public authority to "examine the treatment of persons deprived of their liberty with a view to strengthening, if necessary, the protection of such persons from torture and inhuman or degrading treatment or punishment."[31]

The Committee for the Prevention of Torture (CPT) visited the Russian Federation on nine occasions between December 1998 and May 2002 (see Chapter 8: Asylum-seekers and refugees). All states parties to the treaty have consented to the publication of the CPT visit reports except for the Russian Federation.[32] At the time of writing, therefore, the CPT's findings and recommendations in relation to its visits remain for the most part unknown. However, the CPT's concern over the failure of the Russian Federation to cooperate with the CPT

© School of Peace

In June 2002, 50 Meskhetian families living in Kiyevskaya, Krasnodar Territory, went on a hunger strike in protest at the authorities' failure to grant them citizenship of the Russian Federation, to which they are entitled under federal law. The cards they are holding are headlined "Give the children a passport!" and are addressed to the Minister of the Interior of the Russian Federation, reminding him of the state's obligation to protect the rights of all people living within the Russian Federation.

or implement recommendations made relating to ill-treatment of people detained in a detention facility located at Chernokozovo, a village in the Chechen Republic, from December 1999 to early February 2000, and to take action to investigate and prosecute cases of ill-treatment of people detained in Chechnya during the conflict, led the CPT to make an unprecedented public statement of its concerns.[33]

Amnesty International continues to call on the authorities to authorize publication of the reports of all CPT visits to the Russian Federation and to implement the CPT's recommendations.

In 1993 the Council of Europe set up the European Commission against Racism and Intolerance (ECRI) to combat racism, racial discrimination, xenophobia, anti-semitism and intolerance in all its member states. ECRI carries out its mandate by reviewing states' legislation, policies and other measures to combat racism, and their effectiveness. It proposes recommendations to member states related to policy and action.[34]

To date, ECRI has published two reports on the Russian Federation. In its most recent report in 2001, it noted that the authorities had taken some positive measures aimed at combating racism and intolerance. It also raised concerns about the persistence of discrimination, racism and xenophobia, notably against ethnic and racial minorities, including Chechens, Meskhetians, Ingush refugees, members of the Jewish community and Roma, as well as asylum-seekers and refugees. ECRI recommended to the authorities that "further action be taken to combat racism, xenophobia, discrimination and intolerance in a number of areas."[35] ECRI specifically asked the Russian Federation to:

- ensure that federal legislation and policies aimed at protecting people against discrimination be applied at the regional and local levels;
- review the system of registration of residence and temporary stay and its enforcement procedure in order to ensure that it was not discriminatory in practice;
- counter illegal behaviour on the part of law enforcement officials, particularly against vulnerable groups;
- improve and substantially strengthen the response of the authorities to racial violence and hate speech, including through a more effective implementation of existing legal provisions;
- continue the process of countering extremist political parties and groups; and
- adopt a body of comprehensive civil and administrative anti-discrimination provisions covering discrimination in different fields of life.

© AP

Riot police escort street vendors who do not have appropriate registration papers to a bus to take them to a police station, September 1999.

In the wake of a series of apartment bombings in Moscow and two other cities in September 1999, thousands of "foreigners" were detained and many "deported" to other parts of Russia on the grounds that they had not obtained registration for the city or region in which they were living. In Moscow, the city authorities enforced a secret order requiring all those not permanently registered in the city to re-register within a three-day period.

Chapter 4: Registration – a gateway to abuse

Lom-Ali Tasuev was holding his four-month-old son in his arms when he opened the door to police on 13 September 1999. A computer specialist working in a school, Lom-Ali Tasuev was living in Moscow, where his wife, Khava Tasueva, was registered, even though he was registered in Friazino, a city 25 km from Moscow.

When Khava Tasueva returned home, several men in plain clothes were in the flat carrying out what they said was an "identity check". They told her they were taking Lom-Ali Tasuev to the Liublino police station. When she asked them why, the officers replied, "You are Chechens."

Khava Tasueva and their five children went to the police station, hoping that Lom-Ali Tasuev would soon be released. However, at 11pm the family had to return home without him. Three days later Khava Tasueva was informed that Lom-Ali Tasuev would not be released because 0.15 gm of drugs had been found on him. Khava Tasueva lodged a complaint with the district procuracy and Lom-Ali Tasuev was released on bail shortly afterwards.

According to Lom-Ali Tasuev, five hours after he was detained, during which period he had been searched several times, he was told, in the presence of witnesses, to empty his pockets on to the table. Lom-Ali Tasuev told Amnesty International that an officer looked carefully at the objects, then bent down and pointed to a piece of foil lying under the table. Lom-Ali Tasuev refused to pick it up, saying that it did not belong to him. The foil was found to contain heroin.

Lom-Ali Tasuev's case was heard in Liublino intermunicipal court from 30 November to 1 December 1999. He proclaimed his innocence and stated in court: "I had more than five hours and plenty of opportunity to get rid of anything which could constitute a danger to me, if I had had anything... I have five children, my wife is ill and not working, life is hard for us. What do you think, your honour, could I allow myself to buy an expensive narcotic, and anyway a narcotic for which I have no use whatsoever, not being a drug addict, which is proved by the medical certificate included in the case notes." In an explanation written for the court Lom-Ali Tasuev stated that the drugs were placed on him by the police. He linked the criminal case against him with the anti-Chechen campaign in Moscow which followed a series of bombings of apartment buildings which were blamed by the authorities on "Chechens".

Nevertheless, the judge found Lom-Ali Tasuev guilty, stating that "in unspecified circumstances, at an unspecified time, in an unspecified place Tasuev obtained 0.15 gms of drugs for his personal use from an unspecified person... During a personal search of Tasuev he threw the drug out of his pocket... He says that the police planted the drug, but he did not tell the prosecutor... He confuses his evidence, whereas the evidence of the witnesses [policemen] is coherent, logical and convincing... In the light of his positive character reference, and five children... the court imposes a conditional sentence of six months with one year's probation."

This pattern of targeting members of certain groups for "identity checks", which can then lead to false accusations of and even convictions for criminal activities, continues to this day.

Speaking on International Human Rights Day in December 2001, federal human rights Ombudsman Oleg Mironov identified the processes surrounding residence registration as the most common sphere in which law enforcement officers violated the fundamental human rights of ordinary people.[36] According to Amnesty International's research, it is also the context in which members of ethnic or national minorities are most disproportionately targeted, often leading to arbitrary detention or ill-treatment.

Those living in the Russian Federation are required to register their place of residence with the police. Historically, residence permits were used, both in Soviet and Tsarist times, as a means of restricting movement between countryside and town, and for law enforcement purposes. From 1932 all Soviet citizens aged 16 and above were required to carry an internal passport, which had to bear a stamp (the *propiska*) stating their place of residence. However, Article 27 of the 1993 Constitution guarantees the right of everyone legally resident

Anti-semitic graffiti on the wall of the central office of a Jewish community building in Ulianovsk, in the east of the Russian Federation, April 2002. The graffiti reads "Don't pollute our land".

The failure to investigate and prosecute instances of racist intimidation can leave minority communities at increased risk of violent attacks by giving the signal that racism will be tolerated.

In the town of Tiumen in Siberia, police failed to take action against those responsible for repeated attacks and damage to a synagogue under reconstruction. A group calling themselves the "Tiumen Aryan Skinheads" claimed responsibility on its website for at least one of these attacks in October 2001, making explicitly anti-semitic statements and threatening to burn the synagogue down. The authorities claimed to have identified and even interviewed some of the youths responsible for the October 2001 attack, and the website was eventually closed down. However, no one has yet been charged in relation to the attacks, which the authorities remained reluctant to classify as racist, considering them instead "young people's hooliganism".

A police sentry box was set up near the synagogue, but it was seldom, if ever, staffed.

Finally the attacks on property turned into attacks on the person. In May 2002, three young men emerging from the synagogue were attacked by a group of skinheads, who racially insulted them.

Another member of the community complained to Amnesty International that so far "the advice we have had from [the authorities] is all about what we should do, not what they will do for us. Apparently we are to 'be careful', and not go out alone." She complained that when the young men from her community who were attacked went to give a statement at the police station, the police did not want to write down the racial insults made against them. She felt that the authorities were reluctant to spoil the image of Tiumen by admitting that it harboured racists.

In September 2002 Raphael Goldberg, President of the Jewish Cultural Centre, told Amnesty International that the Russian Federal Prosecutor had instructed the regional prosecutor to pass to him all available information about the attacks.

in the Russian Federation to move freely and to choose their place of residence. Registration, therefore, should entail informing the police of one's address. It should not give the police the opportunity to deny registration to those legally entitled to register.

In practice, in many places, including Moscow and St Petersburg, and the southern regions of Stavropol and Krasnodar, registration procedures require people to seek permission to live at a particular address, rather than just to give information of the fact of one's place of residence. These practices continue despite being contrary to the Constitution, national and international law and Constitutional Court rulings.

Additional restrictions and conditions for registration have been introduced by local governments in the Russian Federation. These open the way for arbitrary decision-making and arbitrary sanctions for violations of the registration regime. Identity checks are often accompanied by bribery, intimidation, extortion and the confiscation of people's identity documents, and frequently result in short-term detention in police stations.

NGOs from the Russian Federation attending the UN World Conference against Racism in 2001 identified the "system of registration and its derivatives as a basic instrument of discrimination and a basic prerequisite for discriminatory practices".[37] They saw the lack of transparency and accountability built into the system as being conducive to discrimination in three key ways:

1   It allowed officials to deny or restrict registration to members of certain ethnic groups;

2   It allowed the person who was denied registration because of their ethnic origin to be deprived of a range of civil rights;

3   It increased the likelihood that those denied registration – and all those who belonged to the particular ethnic group – would be targeted by those "controlling" the system.

This view has been consistently echoed in numerous reports by intergovernmental organizations[38] and international human rights organizations.

Article 11 of the 1991 Law on the Police sets out their responsibilities when checking documents. Paragraph 2 states that the police:

"will check personal identity documents where there are sufficient grounds to suspect that the subject has committed a crime or administrative misdemeanour, and where there are sufficient data to prove that they have about their person arms, weapons, explosives, narcotics or psychotropic drugs, conduct a search of the person, their possessions, hand baggage or luggage, remove these articles..."

Anyone detained in connection with document checks can be held for 48 hours before the case is brought before the prosecutor or a court. Those detained are usually held either in the police station itself or in special detention centres for undocumented persons. Those fined or detained have included people awaiting official decisions as to their legal status, such as asylum-seekers awaiting the decision of the migration service, and non-Russian citizens applying for citizenship.

People who do not have the correct documentation when stopped by police can be fined. They should in return receive documentation stating that they have paid the fine. However, there are numerous reports of police taking the fine and arbitrary amounts in excess of the fine without giving any receipt. According to reports, the only people who have a chance of obtaining an acknowledgement of the fine paid are those who are sufficiently confident of their rights and sufficiently fluent in Russian to demand one. Those who are unable to obtain such documentation are at risk of being serially fined by every police officer met in the course of a day.

Amnesty International is urging the Russian authorities to defend and promote the rights of freedom of movement and freedom from arbitrary detention by taking steps to end the arbitrary, unconstitutional and often racist implementation of registration requirements.

"Whenever a Chechen is late to meet me I start to think: which is the nearest police station?"

Svetlana Gannushkina (*left*) head of the non-governmental organization Civic Assistance which works with asylum-seekers and people displaced by the conflict in Chechnya, or by conflicts in other parts of the Russian Federation and the former Soviet Union.

Alvi Digaev (*right*), a Chechen who fled the Chechen capital, Grozny, to escape the conflict, and Svetlana Gannushkina meet in the offices of Civic Assistance in Moscow which were used to hold classes for Chechen children unable to enrol in school because they and their parents cannot obtain registration in Moscow. Alvi Digaev's 16-year-old daughter has been told that she must return to Grozny if she wishes to obtain a passport.

Chapter 5: Prejudiced policing

Since the start of the second conflict in Chechnya in September 1999, Chechens and other people from the Caucasus living in the rest of the Russian Federation have experienced increasing, if varying, levels of racist attacks and police harassment.

Said-Emin's experience described below mirrors that of Chechens interviewed by Amnesty International at the time of the Moscow bombings in Autumn 1999. The Memorial Human Rights Center, which monitored the outcome of a number of such cases, concluded: "Between fall [autumn] 1999 and spring 2000 there was a veritable campaign of falsification that engulfed the country. The wave returned, on a lesser scale, in August 2000 after a blast in the passage under Pushkin Square in Moscow... The pattern was more or less the same: the police planted drugs, ammunition, hand grenades or explosives during personal searches of Chechens or searches in their flats. The victims were taken to precincts to extort confessions from them. This was crude work yet none of the accused was acquitted. At best defence lawyers managed to insist on further investigation or suspended sentences."[39]

Said-Emin[40] is a Chechen. Between 1988 and 1990 he served in the Russian army in the Moscow region. He has lived in Moscow, where he has worked as a driver, since 1991. His wife, who was born in Moscow, is a shop worker. They have a young son.

On 12 September 1999 Said-Emin returned home from a business trip in Astrakhan after learning that his nine-month-old son was ill. The next day a second bomb exploded in an apartment block in Moscow. The Russian authorities blamed the explosions on "Chechens". The television announced mass round-ups of Chechens in Moscow.[41] Said-Emin's wife persuaded him to leave the city.

Said-Emin told Amnesty International that as he was on his way to his car, police officers stopped him in the hallway of the apartment block. He was searched, his flat was searched and his documents were checked. He was then taken to the local police station, searched again and questioned for four hours. Police at first accused him of taking part in a hotel robbery, and then asked him when he was last in Chechnya.

According to Said-Emin's testimony, he was given something to drink and then questioned about drugs. He said an officer placed a small package of drugs on the table in front of Said-Emin, claiming to have found it on his person. The authorities claimed that a subsequent urine test showed traces of illegal drugs; Said-Emin believes that this must have been the result of whatever was put in the bottle he drank from. Said-Emin told Amnesty International that police officers warned him that if he made a fuss he would receive a longer sentence. In February 2000 Said-Emin was given a six-month suspended sentence for possession and use of drugs[42] and released.

After his release, police reportedly came to Said-Emin's home every week. He told Amnesty International: "There were always five of them with guns. They showed no documents. We did not know their surnames." If he was not at home they would search the flat. Each time they found him at home they would check his papers, including his marriage certificate.

On 7 September 2001 police officers in uniform, accompanied by eight or nine men in civilian clothing, came to Said-Emin's apartment and searched the flat. Said-Emin's wife told Amnesty International that she asked to be allowed to sew up Said-Emin's trouser pockets after they had checked them – a common practice among Chechens, such was the scale of arrests and subsequent accusations relating to possession of narcotics or bullets. The officers refused. Said-Emin was handcuffed and taken to a police station.

At about 2am, three officers entered the room where Said-Emin was being held. One reportedly said, "All you Chechens should be killed", pushed a fist into Said-Emin's front jeans pockets and pulled out a foil packet which the officer claimed contained heroin. Said-Emin says he was then offered a choice: drugs charges or arms charges.

Said-Emin this time refused a police-appointed lawyer and eventually engaged the services of a lawyer of his choice with the help of the NGO Civic Assistance. His lawyer lodged complaints with the general prosecutor over the claims made in a television program that Said-Emin had been detained in the street without documents or registration and in possession of heroin. Said-Emin was released on 10 September 2001. On 8 October he obtained written confirmation that the case had been closed for lack of evidence. Since then, he and his wife have tried to pursue complaints against the police, both in relation to the planting of drugs and the unlawful search of their flat, but without success. The first compliant was turned down "for lack of evidence" and the second has been batted between the different police agencies involved in Said-Emin's arrest. At the time of writing Said-Emin had still not obtained redress.

In general it is difficult to show in individual cases that racist attitudes, policies or procedures lie behind a decision to prosecute, convict, mete out a harsh sentence or deny the right of appeal. On occasion, the racism is revealed – for example by the words of a police officer or judicial official. More often, racism can only be identified by looking at patterns of arrest, conviction and sentencing in relation to the racial background of the defendant or the victim of the crime, the racial background of those involved in administering justice, and so on.

To do this, information relevant to discrimination is needed. In the Russian Federation, the collection of such data is still in its infancy. The difficulty in obtaining such statistical information in itself is a strong indication of deficiency in the justice system. The identification of discriminatory patterns is the first step towards finding ways of combating the discrimination. The government's latest report to the CERD is a welcome start to what should become a useful audit. The Memorial Human Rights Center has also contributed to the identification of such patterns, for example in its 2002 report, *Legal mechanisms for combating ethnic discrimination and incitement to racial hatred in Russia.*

Nevertheless, there are widespread reports of racially discriminatory treatment and bias by police. Many communities report that police unjustly target members of ethnic minorities and automatically see them as potential criminal suspects. There have been a number of reports of law enforcement officials making statements which negatively stereotype certain ethnic or national groups. In the overwhelming majority of instances which have come to Amnesty International's attention, the authorities have failed to act decisively to combat racism of this kind in the administration of justice.

For example, in a submission distributed at the UN World Conference against Racism as part of the contribution of domestic NGOs to that forum, Konstantin Demeter of the

> **"Our national cultural associations think that the fight against drugs is essential for the health of our people... But it is illegal to turn the fight against drugs into incitement of national hatred. Criminals commit crimes not because of their nationality or their belonging to ethnic groups but because of their personal qualities... The main idea is based on these phrases 'We want to stress again the fact that Gypsies, Tajiks, Azerbaijanis and other representatives of ethnic minorities are invaders on our territory.' This is a blatant incitement of national hatred.**
>
> **We are sure that the dissemination of such ideas in the media is illegal, it violates the rights of national minorities and stirs up racial hatred and the growth of national extremism in society. That is why the fight against one crime should not be accompanied by other illegal actions."**
>
> Extract from a letter written in September 2002 to the Ministry of the Press by the Sverdlovsk Oblast branch of the Congress of National Associations, which is made up of leaders from the Chechen, Jewish, Romani, Tajik, Tatar and other minority communities. The letter followed the broadcast on television of an interview with the head of an organization which, according to media reports, used violent methods to combat illegal drug dealing. In the interview he blamed various ethnic minority groups for the drug trade in Yekaterinburg. According to reports, an official warning was issued to this organization and materials relating to the alleged racism were sent to the federal Deputy General Prosecutor.

Romano Khaer Society, Moscow, spoke of the way in which negative stereotypes are created in relation to Roma in the Russian Federation. In 2000, *Argumenty i fakty* (Arguments and facts), a large circulation newspaper, published an article linking Roma with the illegal drug trade.[43] The Moscow City Criminal Investigation Department was quoted as saying that "Moscow gypsies are hereditary actors. They deal in gold and are in the drug business..." The Ministry of the Interior has periodically been reported as mounting anti-crime campaigns in a number of regions of the Russian Federation under the slogan "*Tabor*" (the name for a Romani encampment). The campaigns commonly entail checking the documents of people who answer the stereotypical description of Roma and forcibly relocating them to whatever part of the Russian Federation in which they were last registered.

Discrimination in law and in the administration of justice has dire consequences for the victims of racism. It creates a climate in which both police and members of the public feel they can get away with racist crimes, and in which racial minorities feel unprotected by the state and are left vulnerable to attack.

Racism can pave the way for other human rights abuses such as torture and ill-treatment. Those vilified by nationalist public figures as "the enemy" or as less than human are seen as legitimate targets for human rights abuses simply because of their national, ethnic or religious identity. It is, therefore, of the utmost importance that all law enforcement officials are given a clear message that racism will not be tolerated, and that all allegations of brutality and other human rights abuses made by victims of racism will be thoroughly and independently investigated and the perpetrators brought to justice.

On the morning of 24 January 2001, workers on a construction site in Moscow were anticipating an ordinary working day. The only unusual prospect was that they had been promised by their employers, an Italian construction firm, that they would be paid for the previous three months' work. The workers had downed tools when their employer failed to pay them for the third successive month, and had reportedly agreed to return to work on 24 January after the employer promised to pay them and threatened them with reprisals if they did not turn up for work that day.

According to eyewitnesses, as the men were changing into their work clothes, police officers from RUBOP, the regional organized crime squad, wearing masks and carrying automatic rifles stormed into the building and forced the workers to lie on the floor. They said the officers then began to beat the men to find out who the strike leaders were. The officers reportedly identified Abdullo Vatanov and Rustam Oiakhmadov, both Tajik citizens, as strike leaders, handcuffed them, put several bullets in their pockets, took them to the floor above and severely beat them.

The workers who remained on the floor below were made to stay on the wet cement floor, wearing just T-shirts and work trousers, for three hours in freezing temperatures. The officer opened the windows to increase the workers' discomfort. The men said they could hear Abdullo Vatanov and Rustam Oyakhmadov cry out as they were beaten. The next day the employers reportedly told the workers to leave Moscow immediately unless they wanted the same thing to happen to them.

Abdullo Vatanov and Rustam Oiakhmadov were charged with drugs and weapons offences.[44] During the arrest procedure the two men were questioned by a deputy prosecutor of the Tverskaia Inter-district Prosecutor's Office. Despite their obvious injuries and their allegations that they had been beaten by RUBOP officers, no attempt was made to provide them with immediate medical care.

Two days after their arrest, the newspaper *Sevodnia* (Today) ran a story on the case which prompted the men's lawyer to make an official complaint to the police.[45]

The article claimed that the men had belonged to armed Chechen groups in Chechnya. This story was also broadcast on television. In the context of the anti-Chechen feeling which continued to prevail in Moscow,[46] such allegations could have had very serious consequences for the two men and on whether they obtained impartial and fair treatment by the criminal justice system. According to the two men, they had left Tajikistan in July 2000 and had been working on building sites in Moscow since August 2000. Thanks to the interest taken in the case by the Russian NGO Memorial, who involved lawyer Inna Ailamazian and Deputy of the state *Duma* V.V. Igrunov, the allegations made in the media were challenged.

Despite the defence lawyer's repeated efforts to ensure that witnesses were questioned and medical examinations carried out, she received no response from the authorities. On 14 March 2001 she wrote:

"My attempts to meet with the investigator, [my] requests that the investigator meet the witnesses and have them questioned, and [my attempts to] interview the RUBOP officers who took part in this pogrom, have met with complete failure. At the times set by the investigator for our meeting, the investigator does not appear.

Meanwhile some of the workers, the Tajiks and Moldovans who were eyewitnesses to the pogrom, frightened by the impunity of RUBOP, have left work and left Moscow. The injuries of the accused are fading, so the inactivity of the investigation is inevitably leading to the material

*circumstances of the case being covered up, in some cases
irreplaceably. Since 9 February 2001 when I took on this case,
not a single investigatory action has been undertaken in
relation to my clients, not a single eyewitness to the pogrom
has been questioned..."*[47]

According to the lawyer, no investigative actions had been
undertaken when the Tverskaia Inter-district Prosecutor
prolonged the detention of Abdullo Vatanov and Rustam
Oiakhmadov to 24 April 2001. The two men were subsequently
released on bail, with surety provided by the Tajikistan
embassy.

Inna Ailamazian, who has represented members of ethnic
minorities in similar cases,[48] informed Amnesty International
that she had received a string of suspicious and intimidating
anonymous phone calls which appeared to be connected with
her work on such cases. [49]

© AI

Bektash Fasylov was among five Meskhetians from Krymsk
Region, Krasnodar Territory, who were hospitalized with
concussion after an unprovoked attack by a group of at least 60
self-styled Cossacks in November 2001. There have been many
reports that members of such groups often accompany police on
local operations and conduct raids independently. Official
complaints about the incident were lodged with the police.
However, at the time of writing no one had been brought to
justice for the attack and, according to some reports, the case
had been closed.

"We, inhabitants of the village of Starbeevo, inform you that in May 1999 Tajiks came to our village to work for a telephone company. They set up telephone communications and when the work for that firm was finished, they stayed to do private construction work. Many inhabitants of the village came to them for help with various building jobs. In winter when it froze hard they dug trenches using bonfires. They went out to do the very hardest work, in order to make a living. Among them are people with higher education: a school principal, an engineer, a geologist. With bleeding, calloused hands they honestly earned their own bread. And we, the villagers, with full confidence state that they are completely innocent. They are honest and hardworking people. We, the villagers, who needed help with building jobs, are grateful to these people for their honest, hard work.

Such people earn their money only with the calluses on their hands. We all sign up to their innocence and demand that steps be taken against the excesses committed by the supposed law enforcement agencies..."

Letter to the head of the Main Department of Internal Affairs of Moscow Region and the Prosecutor of the town of Khimki from the inhabitants of the village of Starbeevo, dated 10 July 2000.

On 4 July 2000 a group of unidentified men had entered a house in Starbeevo village, Khimki district, where Tajik construction workers lived, and reportedly insulted and severely beat three men — Azizkhon Davlatov and Samad and Iskandar Ibroimov — before taking them away and charging them with drugs offences. The group also reportedly smashed furniture and removed personal belongings. It subsequently emerged that the men in the group were police officers led by a major from the 4th division of RUBOP, the organized crime squad, in Moscow Region. In March 2002, three officers appeared in court charged with fabricating evidence, exceeding their authority, theft and extortion. At the time of writing in September 2002, the case was pending.

© AI

Two Tajik labourers in the windowless converted garage that serves as their home. They are among the millions of workers from former Soviet republics who have come to the Russian Federation in search of work since 1991. Often the victims of discrimination and vulnerable to exploitation, many have been forced to take low-paid and insecure jobs.

In the Russian Federation many victims of racist torture or ill-treatment do not lodge a complaint. One reason for this is that the victims believe there is little chance of securing a successful conviction of a police officer accused of ill-treatment. Furthermore, victims may not make complaints about certain police "excesses" which do not constitute actual physical ill-treatment, such as racist verbal abuse and threats of violence. Lack of confidence in the justice system is exacerbated by the fact that there is no independent body to review complaints of torture or ill-treatment at the hands of agents of the state.

The authorities have a responsibility to tackle those failures in the criminal justice system which undermine public confidence and reinforce impunity for torturers. The consequence of their failure to live up to this responsibility is that members of ethnic and national minorities remain at risk of abuse by the very forces which should be protecting them.

Chapter 6: 'No one to turn to' – failing to protect

"The worst thing is there is no one to turn to. You call the racism hotline [run by the Moscow authorities] and they just say it is not their region. For example, one time my nephew was stopped by police and told his registration was not in order; they were asking for a 500 ruble [approximately US$16] 'fine'. He called me and I called the hotline. They said it 'wasn't Moscow proper' and so not their concern. Then I called the [Tajik] Embassy... Then I told my nephew to go back to the police station to collect his passport. He had been let out to go and collect money. When he got there he was kicked into a cell and told, 'You know I like money. You are not getting out until I get it.' In the end we had to get the money together and pay."

Bogsho (family name withheld)

Bogsho, a senior member of staff at the Academy of Sciences in Moscow, came to Russia from Tajikistan in 1993. He is a Russian citizen, but this did not protect him from the racist gang that attacked him and his son on 14 May 2002 as they were returning from a cultural event in the Moscow area for people from the Pamir Mountains in Tajikistan.

Just before 5pm between 25 and 30 young skinheads entered the train carriage in which Bogsho, his son and one of Bogsho's students were travelling. They surrounded Bogsho and his companions and started swinging from the bars and kicking them. By the time they reached the next stop, all three victims were covered in blood.

Bogsho told Amnesty International there were two or three young women among the attackers. Some of the attackers took photographs of the three victims lying on the ground while others chanted "Moscow for Muscovites, Russia for the Russians".

When their attackers had left, the three men called the police on a mobile. When no police officers arrived, Bogsho phoned again. The police officer who took the call said that the attackers had not yet been found.

Bogsho and his companions went home and called again. They were told to go to the railway police station at Kuskovo. Bogsho was too badly injured to make the journey, but when he tried to phone the police to tell them this, no one answered.

Bogsho called an ambulance and was taken to hospital where X-rays showed that he had a broken rib. The ambulance crew also called the police.

Three or four days later police officers from Kuskovo arrived at Bogsho's home and asked him for his passport. When Bogsho explained again that he could not come to the station because of his injuries, the officers said they would come back in a day or two. When they finally did return, on 20 May, they reportedly said that there was no point doing anything because the attackers were teenagers.

At the end of May, when Bogsho was sufficiently recovered, he went to the Kuskovo police station. He told Amnesty International that he saw a group of young skinheads marching around waving placards with racist slogans in the park opposite the station. He told the duty officer about the demonstration. The officer did nothing. Bogsho left the station convinced that there was no point in pursuing his case.

States are responsible for protecting people not only against discrimination and torture by their own agents, but also against similar practices by private individuals (non-state actors). The state may be accountable in a number of different ways for attacks by non-state actors. The UN Convention against Torture establishes the responsibility of the state for acts of torture inflicted "with the consent or acquiescence of a public official". For example, failure to provide protection against violent racist attacks may amount to consent or acquiescence in torture.

Under international human rights law, states also have an obligation to act with due diligence to prevent, investigate and hold perpetrators accountable for abuses of human rights, including acts by private individuals. This basic principle of state responsibility is established in all the core human rights treaties to which the Russian Federation is a party. The ICCPR and the European Convention on Human Rights, for example, oblige states to ensure the rights set out in those treaties, including the right to freedom from torture and ill-treatment. The UN Human Rights Committee has stated that this obligation extends to acts inflicted by people acting in a private capacity.[50] The European Court of Human Rights has also affirmed that under the European Convention on Human Rights, states are required to take measures to ensure that individuals are not subjected to torture or inhuman or degrading treatment or punishment, including such ill-treatment inflicted by private individuals.[51]

In addition, the duty of the state to take all appropriate means to prohibit and eliminate racial discrimination by any person, group or organization, including to protect people from violence or bodily harm at the hands of non-state actors, is also expressly set out in the International Convention on the Elimination of All Forms of Racial Discrimination.[52]

The concept of due diligence is a way to describe the threshold of effort which a state must undertake to fulfil its responsibility to protect individuals from abuses of their rights.[53] Due diligence includes taking effective steps to prevent such abuses, to investigate them when they occur, to prosecute the alleged perpetrator and bring them to justice through fair proceedings, and to ensure reparation and other access to effective redress. It also means ensuring that justice is imparted without discrimination of any kind.

"I have filed many cases with the police, but have never got any feedback. Would it make sense to go to the police again?"
A refugee from the Democratic Republic of the Congo speaking about an attack by a gang of youths in April 2002.

Amnesty International considers that acts of violence by private individuals can constitute torture or ill-treatment when they are of the nature and severity envisaged by the concept of torture or cruel, inhuman or degrading treatment or punishment in international standards and when the state has failed to fulfil its obligation to provide effective protection.

Officials often blame racist attacks on young children or drunken teenagers engaged in petty hooliganism. A survey conducted between May 2001 and April 2002 by the Moscow Protestant Chaplaincy's Task Force on Racial Attacks gives a very different picture. The 180 African respondents[54] reported having

© Paula Allen

Adefers and
Sarah Dessu

"This is the wrong place for black skins. But we don't have a place to go, so we stay. We are targeted by racists. Racism is beginning now in a wide way. Before they caught us and beat us. Now they have started killing people... They hang around on every corner. We can't use public transport. They beat us at least three times a year. Since 1996 I have been beaten about 20 times."
Adefers Dessu

Adefers Dessu arrived in the Russian Federation in 1996. He had fled Ethiopia to escape political persecution. In September 2001 he and his wife Sarah were visiting a friend in Moscow who had recently given birth. As they were walking along talking, they were set upon by a gang of about 20 people armed with chains and knives. Adefers Dessu's rib was broken in the attack. He fell to the ground and lost consciousness for a brief period. The attackers then ran off. He told Amnesty International that when the police finally arrived on the scene "[t]he first thing they wanted was our documents. To know who I am. That is Russian 'First Aid'."

To Amnesty International's knowledge, no one has been held to account for this or other assaults on the couple.

Adefers Dessu told Amnesty International: "We want to feel free. We want to go to a free country. In Russia we can see no future. We live by hope but we don't know what is coming. If the militia find a knife or a spray in my pockets they will give me big problems. They will say I am a thief or a criminal 'let's go off for a check'. White people don't get checked. They can defend themselves. They can carry defensive weapons.

We just survive. We survive."[55]

43

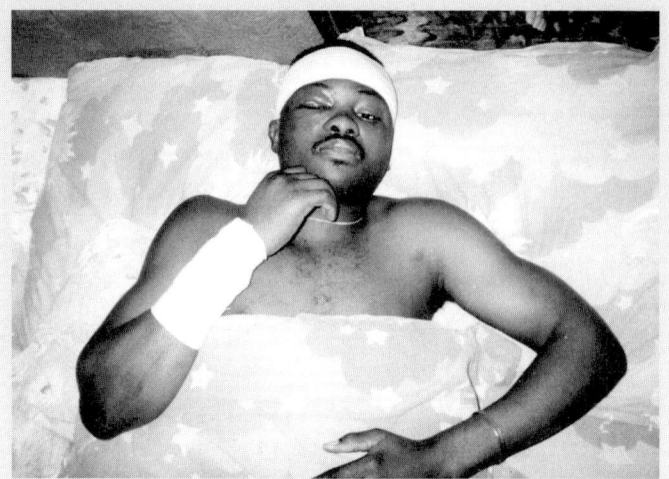

André Guy Tranquille Temgoua, a Cameroonian student, came to the Russian Federation to study in 1996. He told Amnesty International that within a week of his arrival he was attacked by a gang of youths. Since then he has reportedly been attacked on a number of occasions, usually close to the student hostel where he lives, or on his way to university in Moscow. On one occasion he had a toxic gas sprayed in his eyes. He has stated that he has also regularly been subjected to racist insults and threats, including being threatened with a gun in the presence of his Russian wife and son.

He told Amnesty International that despite making official complaints on a number of occasions, the police have concluded either that there were no grounds for opening a case, or that there was no evidence of racial motives.

A survey of Africans living in Moscow, published in 2002 by the Moscow Protestant Chaplaincy's Task Force on Racial Attacks, found that attacks were becoming increasingly life-threatening, with the most common injuries being to the head and face.

suffered 204 attacks during the year, the vast majority carried out by groups. Only four per cent of the attacks reported were carried out by individuals acting alone. Only 13 per cent of victims thought that their attackers were drunk. Sixty-six per cent of victims said that their attackers were armed. None of the attacks was reported to have been carried out by children under 14 (the age of criminal responsibility in the Russian Federation); 54 per cent of respondents said their attackers were adults over 18 years of age.

Of the 204 attacks, only 61 had been reported to the police. Of the 61, only a quarter were actively investigated by the police through, for example, interviewing the victim or witnesses. In only seven per cent of cases were the alleged perpetrators reported to have been prosecuted. Only two cases reportedly resulted in the perpetrators being found guilty of a crime. One of the main reasons given for not reporting assaults, about half of which involved racist verbal abuse as well as violence, was that the victims feared the police would either not recognize their papers issued by the UNHCR, or would use their lack of registration (see Chapter 4) as a reason to detain them and focus on their status rather than on the violent assault they had suffered. The experiences of several of those who did report being attacked shows that these fears were far from groundless.

"I shouted for help and a policeman came. The first thing he did was to ask for my documents."

Ofelia Kofa, a refugee and journalism student from Liberia, speaking of an attack by skinheads in February 2002 when she was alone in the metro.

The authorities in the Russian Federation are failing to ensure effective protection of racial and ethnic minorities from racist attacks by non-state actors. Such attacks are a persistent and increasingly visible factor in Russian society. Amnesty International is calling on the authorities to take urgent steps to ensure the rights of all citizens to be free of racial discrimination. Such steps must include ensuring that the response of the police to victims of racist attacks encourages people to report abuses and does not further undermine confidence in the justice system's willingness or ability to protect them.

© AI

The Aliev family standing outside the original, tumbledown dirt-floor cottage which they bought in the village of Kievskaia in Krasnodar Territory, and next to which they constructed a habitable home. However, they later received notice that their home would be demolished as it had been constructed without official permission.

The authorities' failure to recognize the civil or legal rights of Meskhetians living in Krasnodar Territory means that they are unable to officially register house or land purchases. As a result many are forced to build homes illegally, which leaves them at risk of extortion by corrupt officials or having their homes demolished.

Chapter 7: Racist application of citizenship laws

Lachin Aidinov, a Meskhetian from the village of Novoukrainsk, has lived in the Krymsk District of Krasnodar Territory for more than 12 years. As a Soviet citizen resident in the Russian Federation at the time the Law on Citizenship came into force in 1992, he is entitled to Russian citizenship. However, this right continues to be denied him. The reason is discrimination on the grounds of ethnicity. The result is discrimination in almost every aspect of daily life including education, employment and health care.

Since his arrival from Uzbekistan Lachin Aidinov has applied many times to the Passport and Visa Service of the Ministry of the Interior for documentary recognition of his status as a citizen of the Russian Federation and as a permanent resident in his own home. These applications were all refused, both at local (Krymsk District) and territorial (Krasnodar Territory) level. The refusals were based on Krasnodar Territory laws which contradict federal (national) law.

In September 2001 he went to court and won recognition by the Krasnodar territorial court that he had been permanently resident in the Russian Federation (in Krymsk District) since 1989. However, when he attempted to use this decision to obtain a Russian Federation passport, the Krasnodar Passport and Visa Service turned him down, because he did not have "permanent registration". They also refused to give him "permanent registration".

Lachin Aidinov has made a formal complaint to the Federal Minister of the Interior concerning the actions of the Passport and Visa Service of the Ministry of the Interior in Krasnodar Territory. The outcome was not known at the time of writing.

Lachin Aidinov's situation is typical of that faced by many Meskhetians in Krasnodar Territory, and indeed by others living in regions where unconstitutional local laws on citizenship and registration are in operation.

Meskhetians are a largely Muslim group who were forcibly relocated from southwest Georgia in 1944 by the former Soviet regime. Many Meskhetians who had been transported to Uzbekistan were subsequently forced to flee to Russia in 1989 after violent attacks on them and their property in the Fergana region.[56]

As citizens of the former Soviet Union who were "permanently residing" in the Russian Federation when the Citizenship Law came into force (on 6 February 1992), and who had not declined Russian citizenship, they are by law Russian citizens. There are estimated to be between 50,000 and 70,000 Meskhetians living in the Russian Federation. Most have been able to affirm their right to citizenship. However, the vast majority of the 13,000 to 16,000 Meskhetians living in Krasnodar Territory continue to be denied their legal rights, including their right to citizenship, because of discriminatory legislation and practices in the Territory. In 1999 an estimated 10,000 Meskhetians resident in the Territory remained without registration.[57]

"My son is 20. They won't give him a passport. They give him registration on the basis of a birth certificate. All his documents sat for a year at the passport office. Then they said there would be no more Soviet ones and 'Only citizens get Russian passports'. He can't go anywhere without a passport. Even people with passports get arrested, so what would happen to him?...

If the police go around the houses what am I to do? Hide him? That is why our children are afraid. One ought to go to the police for help, but here we run away...

We have been under house arrest since 1989. It is like living in a prison camp."

Mikhail Madjitov, a Meskhetian living in Krymsk District, Krasnodar Territory, May 2002.

Meskhetians make up around 0.3 per cent of the Territory's five million inhabitants, and between 1.6 and 6.4 per cent of the four local rural districts which they chiefly inhabit.

They are one of several groups who have been denied citizenship in the Russian Federation. A number of ethnic or national minority groups who were citizens of the former Soviet Union and who were forced to move to what became the Russian Federation prior to the collapse of the Soviet Union have found themselves in a similar position, despite legislation which clearly entitles them to citizenship of the Russian Federation. The denial of their basic rights is the result of practices by local authorities who have established their own registration regulations, contrary to federal law. For example, local authorities sometimes insist that citizenship can only be granted to those who had permanent registration (*propiska*) on the day the Law on Citizenship took effect in 1992.[58]

The racial discrimination to which they are subjected in almost every aspect of their lives has been sanctioned by local laws and encouraged by material in the official local media.

"We must protect our land and our native population... from 15 to 20,000 Turks [a term used to denote Meskhetians] are living in Krasnodar Territory, and that is a very serious problem. I say to them, do not forget that you are guests in our land... Some 'guests' are involved in theft, drugs... all available mechanisms of pressure and persuasion will be employed to increase the number of 'guests' leaving. And we should reduce the numbers coming in as well, not only Turks, but Azeris, Kurds and others also."
Governor Tkachev, quoted in the official Krymsk administration newspaper, *Prizyv*, 8 September 2001.

For example, in early 2002 a series of new laws enacted by the Territory's Legislative Assembly overtly aimed to increase pressure on the Meskhetians and other "unwanted" minorities to leave.[59] The passing of these laws, which was widely publicized, coincided with the expiry, or imminent expiry, of the temporary registration held by most Meskhetians.

In February 2002 the legislative assembly of Krasnodar Territory passed a resolution entitled "On further measures to reduce tension in inter-ethnic relations in regions where Meskhetian Turks temporarily residing in Krasnodar Territory are compactly settled".[60] The measures to "reduce tension" are preceded by a paragraph which sets the interests of "citizens of the Russian Federation" against those of the "temporary" Meskhetians. The measures themselves include demanding that the Ministry of Foreign Affairs of the Russian Federation reopen discussions with the authorities in Georgia with the aim of speeding up the return of Meskhetians to "their historic

"If I learn the national anthem, will they leave me alone?"

Zeial, a nine-year-old girl traumatized by a police search of her home for which her parents, obstructed from obtaining official registration in Krasnodar Territory, are unable to acquire valid house and land purchase agreements, May 2002. Her parents had been fined for "illegal land use" and court officials were seeking to confiscate household goods.

Zeial (*left*) and her mother

homeland"; increasing the number of police actions "to identify persons who are illegally on the territory of Krasnodar"; and increasing the number of actions by the Committee on Land Resources "to identify the legality of land allocation and use in areas of compact settlement of ethnic groups" and to "take appropriate measures".

Among other groups affected by such practices are Meskhetians who fled from Uzbekistan in 1989 and 1990 to the Kabardino-Balkarian Republic; some of the Kurds from Armenia and Azerbaijan who sought refuge in Krasnodar Territory, the Republic of Adygeia, and Nizhny Novgorod Region between 1988 and 1990; some of the Armenians who fled from Azerbaijan between 1988 and 1990 to Moscow, Moscow Region, Krasnodar Territory, Stavropol Territory and Rostov Region; and some Ossetians who fled from Georgia between 1990 and 1991 to the Republic of North Ossetia-Alania.

"The Meskhetians are former citizens of the USSR who were legally residing on the territory of the Russian Federation at the time of adoption of the 1992 Citizenship Law. On several individual instances the courts of law, including the Russian Federation Supreme Court, have upheld this position. Without recognition of their citizenship, the Meskhetians live as stateless people. They can face harassment and discrimination..."
UNHCR Moscow, 5 April 2002

The UNHCR has described Meskhetians living in Krasnodar Territory as *de jure* citizens, *de facto* stateless.

Those denied citizenship and permanent registration in the Russian Federation are effectively denied a whole range of basic rights including freedom of movement and equality before the law. Many are arbitrarily deprived of their liberty in the context of police checks on their registration documents; sometimes such checks are carried out by local self-styled Cossacks.[61] Their "statelessness" also expresses itself in denial of access to pensions, child benefits and higher education. They cannot officially register house or vehicle purchases, marriages or deaths. They are frequently stopped and questioned by police on the pretext of checking their identity documentation, and obstructed in their work or going about their daily business.

© AI

Begzadi (*left*) and Sultan Akhmedov

"It was the middle of this month [May 2002]. I was with my parents, Begzadi and Sultan Akhmedov. It was the first time we had dared to go out to work the field. We started to plant too late. After Governor Tkachev [Alexander Tkachev, the Governor of Krasnodar Territory] made that speech saying they would get rid of us in three days no one would sign land use agreements with us, although we had already paid for them. They wouldn't give us back our money either. Some people were advised in Abinsk to put the agreement in the name of a Russian, but we refused to do this.

They must have been watching for when we would start. They reached our field at about 2pm. There were about 15 of them, in three cars, one of them a police car... There was one policeman, representatives of the town administration and tax office of Anapa, and Cossacks dressed in camouflage uniforms and wearing black berets.

They asked for our documents and we showed them. I have had Russian citizenship since 1991. My parents still have their

Soviet passports, issued in Uzbekistan. We came here from Uzbekistan in 1989.

But I am registered in Rostov [a neighbouring region of Russia]. They said, 'Why are you here? You should be in Rostov.' But it is all the same Russia. I am a Russian citizen and I have the right to go wherever I want.

Then they asked for our labour agreement. We don't have one because this year we can't get anyone to give us an agreement. It's not our fault. It's theirs. We explained that we had tried. I said, 'What do you want. Aren't you tired of all this?'

Then they just started telling us to go 'home', saying we did not belong here. All of them were saying this. The Cossacks were the worst, they said, 'We will kick you all out and then put up a monument to ourselves for sorting you out.' They laughed at us, telling us to go to China, Viet Nam, Canada. We said, 'We don't know anything about these countries. We are Soviet people.' They don't think we are human beings.

My parents were terribly upset.

Then they left us, saying they would be back. We had to sign a protocol according to which we have to pay a fine of 1,500 rubles [approximately US$47] for illegal use of land. They said that for every day that we come to work in the field they will take another 1,500 rubles. We asked for their names but they would not give them.

We are still going to go to the field but we don't know what will happen to us. What are we to do? All winter we have to sit at home with no work. What we make from working in the fields in the summer is all we have to live on during the year.

If you write about us, use our names. Everything that I have said is the truth."
Gulia Ishikhova

Gulia Ishikhova and her parents were interviewed by an Amnesty International delegate in May 2002 in Varennikovskaia village and nearby fields. At the time of the interview the family's three-month registration was due to expire on 1 June. They, along with thousands of other Meskhetians, were afraid that the initiatives of the local legislators of Krasnodar Territory meant that their temporary registration would not be renewed and they would be forcibly removed from the region. In the event, a further period of temporary registration was given, which merely ensures that the Meskhetians remain in the vulnerable position which has been their lot for 13 years.

According to expert legal opinion,[62] under the terms of the federal Constitution only the Russian federal authorities have the right to make laws in matters relating to freedom of movement. This has not, however, prevented such laws from being enacted in a number of regions including Krasnodar Territory. The Constitutional Court has reviewed the practice of enforcement by various local authorities of registration procedures and found them unconstitutional.[63]

Furthermore, experts consider that legislation enacted by the authorities in Krasnodar Territory directly contradicts the federal Constitution and federal law in a number of ways, opening up the opportunity for discrimination and corrupt practices. These include:

- Adapting Article 27 of the federal Constitution so that citizens' right to move "freely" within the Russian Federation is restricted to a right to move "in accordance with existing legislation".[64]

- Establishing local Commissions of Migration Control to decide who has the right to be in the Territory, undermining the right of all those legally in the Russian Federation to be in any part of the Federation, including Krasnodar Territory.[65] These Commissions have unlimited power to grant or deny people the right to live permanently in the territory.[66]

- Decisions on whether a person may be in the Russian Federation and for what period can only be taken by the federal authorities. However, the Law of Krasnodar Territory limits registration of foreigners and stateless people to one period of a maximum of 90 days.[67]

- The areas of the Federation classified as "border zones", and therefore subject to restricted access, are defined in the federal law. Krasnodar Territory is not defined as a "border zone" in federal law, but appears to define parts of the Territory as a "border zone" in local law.[68]

- Only federal law can restrict rights and freedoms in order to protect the foundations of constitutional order, the morals, health, rights and interests of others, to ensure the defence of the country and security of the state. However, the authorities of Krasnodar Territory claim for themselves the power to impose such restrictions "to the extent necessary".

Amnesty International has received reports from elsewhere in the Russian Federation of individuals being denied access to procedures for acquiring the citizenship to which they are legally entitled where racial discrimination appears to be a determining factor in the treatment meted out by the authorities.

© AI

Brice Ewalaka-Koumou

Brice Ewalaka-Koumou is from the Republic of the Congo. Article 18(a) of the Law on Citizenship should give him an entitlement to citizenship of the Russian Federation because he is married to a Russian citizen. The student visa on which he entered Russia has expired. The couple have a young son who is still suffering from the trauma of Brice Ewalaka-Koumou's arrest and detention in October 2001. This followed attempts by Brice Ewalaka-Koumou and his wife to lodge his application for citizenship in January 2001. The application was not even accepted. On the second attempt Brice Ewalaka-Koumou and his wife were fined and his identity papers were confiscated. Brice Ewalaka-Koumou claims that he was not informed that the authorities issued an order for his deportation on 15 February 2002 and an order for his arrest and forcible return on 20 July 2002. Brice Ewalaka-Koumou told Amnesty International:

"At 7pm on 18 October 2001, I was invited to come to the police station (No. 20) with my wife. We had our son with us, who is now three; he celebrated his birthday without me while I was in prison. We were told to go and see the head of the station. His deputy was there. He told us to wait. We sat and waited. Then a police officer came and said, 'They have asked you to come; they need to check some documents'."

Brice Ewalaka-Koumou, his wife and son were reportedly driven to a reception and distribution centre where they were told that he was to be deported. The couple asked to see the documents ordering the forcible return. The officers reportedly refused and told Brice Ewalaka-Koumou's wife: "If you aren't satisfied, you're just an enemy to your people anyway and you'll be kicked out too." They were not allowed to call a lawyer.

*"They told me to give them all my personal property. I said I
wanted to give it to my wife. Then they told me to take off my
belt and shoelaces. I said 'At least let my family go, don't
traumatise my child.' My son was crying. I told my wife to call
my friends at Union africaine [an NGO run by Africans resident in
St Petersburg] and a lawyer.*

*"They wanted to put me in handcuffs. When I asked why
they said it was because I might escape. Why would I escape? I
am not a criminal."*

Brice Ewalaka-Koumou was taken by car to the reception
and distribution centre of the GUVD (Main Department of
Internal Affairs). On 27 November Brice Ewalaka-Koumou's
lawyer, Olga Osipova-Tseitlina, saw him. Only then did Brice
Ewalaka-Koumou learn that a court had, in his absence, agreed
that he should be held for a further 90 days beyond the initial
48 hours. He remained in custody until 17 January 2002.

*"On 17 January 2002 at 12.00 midday they told me I was
free. I asked for a document to say I had been released from
there. They refused. I said I looked all dirty and would get
picked up by the police in the street. I was given no
documentation. I was told to go to OVIR [the Department for
Visas and Registration] myself to get my passport. I asked to
be allowed a call to my wife. They told me to call from the
street..."*

At the time of writing Brice Ewalaka-Koumou had applied to
the Federal Migration Service for temporary asylum while his
court cases are pending and he was awaiting an appeal hearing
on his citizenship application.[69] OVIR was reported to have
rescinded the deportation order.[70]

The federal authorities have a responsibility to combat
discrimination whether it emanates from discriminatory laws or
sub-legislative acts at the regional level or from the
discriminatory implementation of federal or local laws. It is time
that the government took decisive steps to put a halt to
measures which breach both the laws and Constitution of the
Russian Federation and its international commitments to
combat discrimination.

СТОЙКОСТЬ

МУЖЕСТВО

НАДЕЖДА

ОТМЕЧАЕМ
ВСЕМИРНЫЙ ДЕНЬ БЕЖЕНЦЕВ

20 ИЮНЯ

УВАЖЕНИЕ

A leaflet produced in the Russian Federation by the UNHCR for World Refugee Day,
20 June 2002. The text reads: "Strength, courage, hope, respect".

Chapter 8: Asylum-seekers and refugees

Samuel Davies, a 34-year-old community health nurse from Sierra Leone, arrived in Moscow in 1993. In February 1995 he registered with the UNHCR for refugee status. In Sierra Leone he had been a youth officer in an opposition party. He told Amnesty International that he had fled his home after his father was executed in 1992 for involvement in a failed coup plot and after his brother was abducted following an attack on the family home in February 1992.

On 16 March 2001 Samuel Davies was approached by three police officers who asked for his documents. He showed them the document he had received on registering with the UNHCR. Samuel Davies told Amnesty International, "the policeman was aggressive and said 'this is not a real document; it's toilet paper. Have you money for a fine?' I had none."

Samuel Davies was taken to the police station (located in Block 8 of the Russian University of Peoples' Friendship) where he says he was held for four days without food. He reports that he was only fed when an immigration officer was due to see him. There were no blankets or bedding in the cell. Samuel Davies told Amnesty International: "You have to ask to go [to the toilet] and if they are in a bad mood they will just tell you to forget about it." No telephone call was allowed.

An immigration officer interviewed him on 20 March and promised to contact the UNHCR. On 28 March Samuel Davies was sent to the Severnyi camp, the main detention centre for "illegal" male foreign nationals in Moscow.

Samuel Davies told Amnesty International that at Severny he shared cells with people from Angola, Cameroon, China, Congo, Georgia, Nigeria and Viet Nam; most detainees were from Viet Nam and former Commonwealth of Independent States (CIS)[71] countries. He described the camp as divided into two sections: one for Russian nationals and the other for foreign nationals. Russian nationals brought to Severnyi for vagrancy or "homelessness" are generally held for around 10 days; foreign nationals can be held for as long as two years without charge or trial. Samuel Davies remained in Severnyi for more than 10 months. He was released following intervention by the UNHCR. On his release he required treatment for tuberculosis which he says he contracted in Severnyi.

He told Amnesty International, "If you had no friends to help you would die. Even if they bring things in for you, you don't get them all. If you complain there are merciless beatings." [72]

Samuel Davies told Amnesty International that he was detained again on 21 May 2002. As before, the detention occurred in the context of a document check. He reports that after he produced his papers, the officer became abusive and threatened that he would make sure Samuel Davies left the country.

The procedure to determine refugee status which is currently in force had not been implemented at the time of Samuel Davies' arrival in the Russian Federation. However, the problems he experienced in asserting the legality of his asylum-seeker status persist under the new law and procedure.

Asylum-seekers are frequently left without recognized identity documents for months or even years, waiting for their claims for protection to be examined. Those who are detained for not having recognized identity documents can be held indefinitely on the basis of a court decision as "illegal aliens" in reception and distribution centres pending deportation. [73]

The UNHCR has registered 40,000 asylum-seekers, predominantly from Africa, the Middle East and Asia, in the Russian Federation since 1992. However, the UNHCR estimates that only 500 individuals from non-CIS countries have been granted asylum by the Russian federal authorities over the past five years. Until very recently the rejection rate at Sheremetevo II international airport in Moscow was reported to be 100 per cent.

Asylum-seekers are often harassed and ill-treated by law enforcement officers who feel they can abuse such people with impunity. Amnesty International has received persistent reports of asylum-seekers from outside the territory of the former Soviet Union having their identity papers destroyed by police and being subjected to police harassment in the form of extortion, beatings and general intimidation. Many have been subjected to police raids or intimidated into leaving their homes.

People who have fled to the Russian Federation from countries where human rights abuses are widespread are at risk of being forcibly returned, in violation of the UN Convention relating to the Status of Refugees, to which the Russian Federation is a party. They are also at constant risk of being detained in violation of international human rights standards. Amnesty International believes that if someone is deprived of their liberty, whether in a prison, detention centre, a closed camp or any other restricted area, that person must be considered to be in detention. The detention of asylum-seekers is allowed by international standards only:

- if it is necessary, and
- if it is lawful, and
- if it is for one of the following reasons:
  (i) "to verify identity";
  (ii) "to determine the elements on which the claim to refugee status or asylum is based";
  (iii) "to deal with cases where refugees or asylum-seekers have destroyed their travel or identity documents or have used fraudulent documents in order to mislead the authorities of the State in which they intend to claim asylum";
  (iv) "to protect national security or public order".[74]

These conditions place the onus on the detaining authorities to demonstrate why other measures short of detention are not sufficient. Moreover, even if an asylum-seeker is detained, detention should be proportionate and reasonable in the individual case. The decision to detain should be subject to automatic and regular periodic review before a judicial or administrative body independent of the detaining authorities.[75] In practice, the decision to detain asylum-seekers is often arbitrary, resting on factors such as the attitude of the official involved to the ethnic origin of the asylum-seeker, rather than on an objective assessment of whether detention is actually necessary and justified. According to reports, asylum-seekers and refugees deprived of their liberty are often held in conditions that amount to cruel, inhuman or degrading treatment.

Article 4 of the 1997 Law on Refugees provides for a preliminary examination to decide on the admissibility of the refugee claim. The most commonly applied restrictions during this preliminary examination are the following:

- Under the terms of Article 5.1.5 of the 1997 Law, if a person arrives from a foreign state in whose territory the applicant had the opportunity to be recognized as a refugee, this can be a ground for not proceeding to examine the applicant's substantive case for asylum. The migration service has commonly failed to investigate the genuine nature of that "opportunity", including whether the state in question is prepared to readmit the asylum-seeker.
- Under the terms of Article 5.1.7 of the 1997 Law, failure to submit a refugee application within 24 hours, if the asylum-seeker crossed the border into the Russian Federation illegally, is also a ground for not considering an asylum application on its merits. Many asylum-seekers do not know of the possibility of making such an application until beyond the first 24 hours. Russian refugee bodies are not represented in all parts of the country and NGOs able to provide the type of guidance needed are few and far between.

The majority of asylum applications are lodged in Moscow City and Moscow Region. According to the UNHCR's monitoring of refugee status determination procedures in these localities, the time limit to submit a claim and the "safe third country" rule account for more than 50 per cent of decisions that asylum applications are not admissible. The total rejection rate, according to the UNHCR's Moscow Office, is 96 per cent.

> *"A refugee is a non-citizen of the Russian Federation who, owing to a well-founded fear of being persecuted for reasons of race, religion, citizenship or nationality (ethnic origin), membership of a particular social group or political opinion, is outside the country of his nationality and is unable or, owing to such fear, is unwilling to avail himself of the protection of that country; or, possessing no definite nationality and who, not having a nationality and being outside the country of his former habitual residence as a result of such events, is unable or, owing to such fear, unwilling to return to it".*
>
> Article 1, para. 1 of the Russian Federation Law on Refugees of 1997

The Federal Migration Service (FMS) was established by decree in 1992. At the time of writing, it had only existed in its latest incarnation within the Ministry of the Interior for seven months. Between May 2000 and October 2001 it had been located within the Ministry for Nationalities. Like its predecessors, the FMS in the Ministry of the Interior bears responsibility not only for refugee matters but also for labour migration and displaced persons.

The Russian NGOs dealing on a day-to-day basis with asylum-seekers, such as Civic Assistance in Moscow, have expressed concern that the Ministry of the Interior, which is most closely identified with the problematic face of policing in the Russian Federation, was an inappropriate body to be given responsibility for dealing with issues of asylum. They have also expressed concern that the FMS's current location could perpetuate the practice of seeing asylum as just another element of migration control. However, some others have hoped that this new location might introduce order into an area whose failures in recent years could be interpreted as a product of poor management, coupled with weak state and legal authority, as much as any deliberate policy on the part of the government to prevent refugees from seeking protection in the Russian Federation.

Recent public pronouncements on the work of the FMS have tended to concentrate on the need for an incoming workforce in the face of Russia's shrinking population and the need to ease the return of ethnic Russians wishing to return from the CIS and other countries. The Ministry of the Interior has estimated that in 2002 it was responsible for dealing with some 10 to 12 million "foreigners" residing unofficially or illegally in the Russian Federation.[76] For most of its history the FMS has had a backlog of non-CIS asylum-seekers, the majority of whom come to Moscow or St Petersburg. Since 1992 the UNHCR has registered 40,000 such asylum-seekers, and continues to register around 20 a month.[77] It is safe to say that the concept of asylum is not widely known or understood in the Russian Federation.

In response to this situation the UNHCR runs a Refugee Reception Centre for non-CIS asylum-seekers. After a preliminary interview asylum-seekers are registered with the UNHCR and provided with legal advice throughout the refugee

Although the 1997 Law on Refugees provides for a preliminary review of the asylum-seeker's case to be undertaken by the FMS within five days of submission of the asylum application, in practice applicants have been put on a waiting list and given a date to formally submit their applications. This date could be as long as 18 months later. During the waiting period, asylum-seekers remain without any officially recognized document attesting to their status.

Once they have submitted their applications, asylum-seekers are supposed to receive an asylum-seeker certificate within 24 hours. In practice they receive a letter of attestation which is not recognized by the law enforcement agencies as being a legal basis for registration and, therefore, for temporary legalization of the asylum-seeker's stay in the Russian Federation.

Lack of officially recognized documentation is the common fate of both CIS and non-CIS asylum-seekers, although, as described elsewhere, the consequences of lack of documentation impact more on those most easily identifiable as "alien" and those furthest from the help of traditional support structures.

Under Article 7 of the 1997 Law on Refugees, the FMS should reach a decision on the merits of the asylum application within three months of recognizing its admissibility, a period which can be, and commonly is, extended for a further three months. This can leave asylum-seekers for up to two years without any recognized legal document which entitles them to stay in the country. As a result they cannot obtain registration or access the social benefits which derive from registration, such as medical care and education. They are subject to fines and detention by the police and have no protection against deportation. The UNHCR is aware of the forcible return of asylum-seekers from Severnyi.[78]

status determination procedure conducted by the FMS, including at the appeal stage. The UNHCR issues registration letters which take the place of the asylum-seekers' certificates which the FMS has yet to issue. These letters are not recognized by the authorities as having any legal status. The UNHCR letters should provide some degree of protection against police harassment, especially during the initial period – which usually lasts some 18 months – during which asylum-seekers do not even have a letter of attestation from the FMS. The UNHCR also provides medical care and education to replace the state benefits from which asylum-seekers are excluded by their lack of legal documentation from the Russian Federation authorities.

In March 2000 people recognized by the FMS as refugees began to receive a refugee certificate which, under Article 7 of the 1997 Law on Refugees, should be valid for three years, with the possibility of extension on a yearly basis. The certificate was not issued before this date mainly because, according to the law enforcement ministries, it was susceptible to forgery.

However, to date those in possession of such refugee certificates have not automatically been able to obtain registration. In some cities and regions, additional requirements have been imposed for the granting of registration which go beyond the limits of police control in the registration process that were clearly defined under the Constitutional Court's decision of 2 February 1998. The additional requirements imposed for registration can include the presence of close relatives legally residing in the city or region, the payment of high fees, and the availability of a minimum amount of square metres per person. As a result, recognized refugees can again be denied access to civil, economic and other rights. (See Chapter 4: Registration – a gateway to abuse, for more information on registration and the additional requirements imposed in parts of the Russian Federation.)

Those appealing against a negative decision by the FMS also face delays and discrimination. In law, the appeal has a suspensive effect; that is, asylum-seekers cannot be deported until an appeal has been heard. However, in practice, this is often ignored so that the asylum-seeker is at risk of deportation. Until October 2000, appeals by asylum-seekers were heard by an FMS appeals commission. This commission would take around 18 months to hear appeals during which time the asylum-seeker was without recognized legal documentation attesting to their status. In October 2000 the appeals commission's activities were suspended, giving rise to yet further delays. Appeals to the courts against a negative decision by the commission should be heard within six months. However, the FMS is required to be represented in court and its failure to attend in many instances again gives rise to further delays during which the asylum-seeker has no recognized legal documentation. In several cases where the FMS's decision was overturned, the FMS appealed the case, again resulting in more delays and extending the period of time during which the asylum-seeker is without legal documentation.

An Iranian national arrived at Moscow's Sheremetevo II
international airport in March 2001 seeking asylum. He
attempted to apply for refugee status at the immigration control
point inside the airport, but on 15 March was told that his claim
would not be considered. An appeal against this decision was
lodged with the court on 28 March. Meanwhile he was detained
at the private detention facility run by Aeroflot, a private airline
of which the majority shareholder is the Russian government, in
the Sheremetevo Hotel.

Despite the fact that the Moscow Office of the UNHCR
informed all the relevant authorities and the airline that an
appeal was pending, and despite assurances given by Aeroflot
that the asylum-seeker would not be deported, the man was
forcibly returned to Iran. His forcible return breached national
law and the fundamental principle of "*non-refoulement*" in
international law.[79] According to information received by
Amnesty International, he was arrested on his return to Iran.

Asylum-seekers arriving at Sheremetevo II international
airport usually fly in on Aeroflot flights from Africa, the Middle
East and Asia. They face immediate forcible return by the airline
unless they find and are able to approach the immigration
control point in the transit area (which at the time of writing
was only open on weekdays; there is a 24-hour immigration
office outside the transit zone), or manage to place a call to the
UNHCR's Moscow Office, a friend or an NGO.

In recent years the immigration control point has tended to
inform UNHCR of all those refused substantive examination of
their case, enabling UNHCR to interview them and, where
necessary, to appeal against that decision. The authorities have
also cooperated with UNHCR regarding the training of FMS staff.

Those who arrive without identification documents on
Aeroflot flights and cannot be immediately returned are dealt
with by Aeroflot.[80] This private company, not a state body,
maintains a detention facility in Sheremetevo II international
airport consisting of nine rooms on the eighth floor of the
Sheremetevo Hotel. Aeroflot is responsible for the costs related
to the accommodation and removal of undocumented
passengers. UNHCR has made repeated suggestions, most
recently to the Head of the Migration Unit in the Office of the
Human Rights Ombudsman,[81] that responsibility for custody of

undocumented passengers be transferred to a state body. This would remove the current possibility of a conflict of interest.

The UNHCR has issued advice, in principle, not to apply the "safe third country" notion to asylum-seekers who have stayed in, or transited, the Russian Federation owing to "serious risk of refoulement and considering the current difficulty for returned asylum-seekers to have access to the refugee determination procedure".[82]

An anti-fascist demonstration in St Petersburg. The demonstration took place on 8 May 2001, the day before Russia celebrates the anniversary of Nazi Germany's capitulation in 1945.

Chapter 9: Recommendations to the government of the Russian Federation

Amnesty International calls on the government of the Russian Federation to commit itself, in word and action, to ensuring respect, protection and promotion of the human rights of all people in the Russian Federation.

It calls on the authorities to give an unequivocal message that violations of these rights will not be tolerated and to ensure that victims of abuses have ready access to effective redress and reparation. It calls for the perpetrators of such abuses to be brought to justice in fair proceedings. It calls on the authorities to ensure that strategies and plans to combat human rights abuses contain measurable goals and monitoring mechanisms.

Amnesty International believes that the implementation of the following measures would radically improve the protection of the human rights of minorities, including combating discrimination on grounds of race, in the Russian Federation.

1. Combat racism and promote tolerance and respect for difference

In the context of the State Program on Tolerance and Prevention of Extremism in Russian Society, review curricula and teaching methods in order to eliminate prejudices, racist attitudes and negative stereotyping. Ensure that representatives of affected groups, relevant NGOs and reputable experts working on the issue of racism, as well as relevant officials, are involved in this process.

Institute comprehensive and continuing training and performance monitoring programs to ensure that public officials, including law enforcement officials, border officials, members of the security forces, judges and lawyers, including prosecutors, do not themselves act in a discriminatory way and are aware of their obligation to protect all people from such discriminatory action by others. This training should be in line with Amnesty International's 12-Point Guide for Good Practice in the Training and Education for Human Rights of Government Officials (see Appendix I) and with CERD's General Recommendation XIII on the training of law enforcement officials in the protection of human rights.[83]

Take urgent measures to address and counter widespread sentiments of hostility and high levels of prejudice against ethnic or national minorities, and in particular ethnic Chechens. Strengthen efforts to counter the phenomenon of racial slurs and exploitation of anti-semitic feeling.

2. Stop racist implementation of citizenship and registration regulations

Undertake a thorough review of legislation, regulations and practices at both federal and regional levels with the aim of removing any elements of the passport and registration process which impact disproportionately, or lead to systematic discrimination against, particular minority groups. Include in such a review all normative acts, instructions or orders concerning passport and registration controls.

Take urgent steps to ensure that all those who are entitled to citizenship of the Russian Federation – including Meskhetians in Krasnodar Territory – are not denied their legal right to citizenship because of discriminatory legislation, regulations or practices.

3. Combat prejudiced policing

Establish a system guaranteeing that complaints of discriminatory behaviour exhibited by the police and other officials are investigated thoroughly, promptly, transparently and independently. Ensure that the system is widely publicized.

Ensure that officials under investigation are suspended from their positions of responsibility pending the outcome of the investigation and any disciplinary and/or judicial proceedings against them.

Ensure that those lodging complaints of discrimination, witnesses and others involved receive protection against any form of intimidation, harassment or abuse and that they are kept informed of the progress of the investigations.

4. Protect ethnic or racial minorities from torture and ill-treatment

Ensure that where there are reasonable grounds to believe that assaults are racially motivated, they are investigated and prosecuted as such.

Ensure that all allegations of torture or ill-treatment by private and semi-official individuals and groups are promptly, thoroughly and impartially investigated and that the perpetrators of such abuses are brought to justice.

Ensure that all allegations of torture or ill-treatment by agents of the state are subjected to prompt, thorough, effective and impartial investigations and that the perpetrators are brought to justice.

Take all other measures necessary to prevent and punish torture including those set out in Amnesty International's 12-Point Program for the Prevention of Torture by Agents of the State, which is set out in Appendix II.

Ensure that victims of torture or ill-treatment have access to reparation, including compensation, medical care and rehabilitation.

5. Protect ethnic and racial minorities from arbitrary detention

Ensure that no one is detained except in accordance with procedures and for reasons established by national and international law and standards.

Ensure that all detainees, including migrants without recognized identity or registration documentation, are immediately informed, in a language they understand, of the reason for their detention. They should also be informed of their rights to lodge complaints about their treatment, to be brought promptly before a court and to have a judge rule without delay on the lawfulness of their detention. Ensure that the legality and necessity of continued detention are regularly reviewed by a court in the presence of the detainee.

In the context of persistent allegations that criminal cases have been fabricated against members of ethnic and racial minorities in order to discredit or punish such groups, conduct a review of disputed cases brought under Article 222 (illegal weapons) and Article 228 (illegal drugs) of the Criminal Code.

6. Protecting asylum-seekers, refugees, migrants and internally displaced people

Take immediate steps towards establishing and implementing a fair and satisfactory refugee determination procedure that no longer leaves foreign nationals vulnerable to arbitrary detention and ill-treatment or *refoulement*.

Take immediate steps to ensure that harassment, arbitrary detention or ill-treatment of asylum-seekers by police are stopped. Specific and clear instructions regarding the treatment of asylum-seekers and respect for UNHCR registration documents should be issued to all law enforcement personnel. Those who do not comply with these instructions should face appropriate disciplinary proceedings and/or prosecution.

Ensure that asylum-seekers are provided with full information on their procedural rights at all ports of entry, in a language they understand. They should be informed of their right to contact the UNHCR, NGOs and legal counsel.

The government should ensure that the UNHCR has free and unhindered access to the transit zone of the airport, as well as any facility where undocumented passengers may be detained.

Ensure that a state body is directly responsible for the decision to detain foreign nationals.

Ensure that people who have fled the conflict in Chechnya are not returned to Chechnya or other parts of the Russian Federation unless and until their safe and durable return with dignity is assured.

7. Identify discriminatory patterns

Ensure that crimes which there are reasonable grounds to believe are racially motivated are classified and prosecuted as such.

Analyse how race and ethnicity may be a factor influencing the reasons and circumstances for a person's arrest and detention.

Record and review police, prosecutorial and judicial responses to complaints of racially discriminatory treatment to examine how race and ethnicity may be a factor influencing the relevant body's response to such complaints, and make public the conclusions.

Ensure that official statistical reports include data on the number and results of hearings in civil, as well as administrative and criminal cases arising in relation to incitement to racial, national or religious hatred.

Take steps to ensure that government monitoring agencies, including ombudsmen's offices, and the police publish regular statistical data on the type and outcome of complaints of discriminatory behaviour and disciplinary action taken.

8. Strengthen the effectiveness of international protection

Ensure dissemination throughout the Russian Federation of the conclusions and recommendations of the UN CERD. Ensure the recommendations are implemented through concrete and comprehensive plans, including measures for regular and continuous monitoring of their implementation.

Authorize publication of the reports of all visits made by the CPT to any place in the Russian Federation. Ensure the publication and dissemination of reports and recommendations by ECRI.

Issue a standing invitation to all UN special procedures, and in particular to the Special Rapporteur on contemporary forms of racism, racial discrimination, xenophobia and related intolerance.

Ratify Protocol No. 12 to the European Convention on Human Rights.

Promote good practice in the training of public officials in international human rights standards using experience and best practice derived from existing international training programs conducted by the UNHCR, Council of Europe, International Committee of the Red Cross (ICRC) and national and international non-governmental organizations.

Recommendations to the international community

States should refrain from returning asylum-seekers to the Russian Federation on the basis that it is a "safe third country" until such time that all asylum-seekers are assured of an

opportunity to have their refugee status determined in a fair
and satisfactory procedure and have access to adequate
protection, including access to durable solutions.

Maintain and expand appropriate assistance programs in the
area of human rights and in particular in the area of promotion
and protection of the rights of ethnic, national or racial
minorities, emphasizing the importance of involving civil
society, including representatives of minority communities, in
delivery and monitoring.

Ensure that people who have fled the conflict in Chechnya
are not returned to Chechnya or other parts of the Russian
Federation unless and until their safe and durable return with
dignity is assured.

Appendix I: A 12-Point Guide for Good Practice in the Training and Education for Human Rights of Government Officials

1) Prior assessment of the human rights situation is absolutely vital.

Before starting a human rights training program it is essential to determine whether it is feasible in light of the human rights situation in the particular country.

A needs assessment should also be carried out so as to identify priority objectives and determine the scope and approach of the program. The human rights problems faced by civil society should be a determining factor of the kind of training to be provided and the government institutions which should be involved.

In some cases the prior assessment may conclude that training does not make sense as an initial step due to the seriousness and nature of the human rights violations taking place — for example because there is a pattern of impunity or because human rights violations are committed by military or paramilitary groups which training could not reach, or when the ministry in question is in such disarray that other steps are needed before the introduction of human rights issues into the curricula can be made effective.

In such cases it may be considered inappropriate to provide training to national officials until laws which fail to satisfy minimum international and regional standards are amended or repealed, prison conditions improved or certain types of security forces (such as paramilitary groups) abolished.

Lobbying, including training on how to carry out legislative changes, may be more constructive than general training on human rights issues in a first instance — training could even be counter-productive if the circumstances are not appropriate.

Even in the worst of situations the above considerations should not preclude the need to implement human rights awareness raising campaigns which, for example, may include public seminars or round tables that point out the need for human rights development and consistency with human rights norms.

2) Human rights education should be one step towards achieving greater accountability.

Human rights training will be most effective where the authorities are committed to upholding human rights standards and government officials are open to scrutiny.

In a country where human rights violations are systematic, unless the government undertakes to change its overall policy in relation to human rights, training runs the risk of becoming just a drop in the ocean. Several governments have boasted about their training programs but these do not seem to have led to an improvement in the overall human rights situation in the country. Governments should assume the responsibility to provide quality programs, support, adequate resources and follow-up.

Human rights training will not be effective if developed in isolation; instead training must be one more step towards achieving greater accountability. Government officials should be made aware that their conduct cannot evade scrutiny by agreeing to initiate training programs.

Governments should also give visible signs of their commitment to human rights. For example by supporting changes in the legislation, allowing freedom of expression and association, initiating their own events and backing events in support of human rights organized by social groups, or by implementing nationwide public education campaigns on human rights.

In some cases human rights training conferences and seminars could play a key role in bringing about reforms by stimulating carefully targeted groups. For example, jurists and politicians both have high public visibility and participate in decision-making which affects the application of human rights standards.

Training and education should be part of a comprehensive human rights strategy and fit into a broader framework of human rights reform.

3) Officials should commit themselves to implementing the training program as an essential part of their profession.

The adequacy of training programs and the integration of human rights concerns into the curricula is the overall responsibility of the government. The implementation of human rights standards must be critical factors in determining promotion and assignments.

The relevant officials should be assigned and assume responsibility for the overall administration of human rights programs and must have support at the highest possible level. It might be preferable to first make changes in the local legislation to ensure the commitment of the authorities and the long-term sustainability of the human rights education (HRE) program.

4) The training program must be coordinated with other human rights activities in the government institutions and in the community.

Human rights training programs should not just provide one-off training courses for selected officials but should establish a sound national training structure and contribute to the creation of a national culture of respect for human rights, involving both the sector in question and those sectors of society it is supposed to serve. For example, the police as well as social workers, in countries where there are children living on the streets, should be encouraged to engage in dialogue with the children so as to gain better understanding of the needs and difficulties they face, and at the same time tackle prejudices which often are at the root of violent responses.

5) Non-governmental organizations should play a key role at all stages of the training program.

When determining the suitability of the country for human rights training it is of crucial importance to consult with local NGOs over the objectives, and the design of the program, in the administration and follow-up of the program and in the evaluation of the program. It could prove extremely valuable to involve NGO trainers so that much-needed dialogue with the government can be established – in this way fomenting a new and different partnership within what until now might have been a relationship of aggression and mistrust.

Where NGOs cannot or will not undertake to train, they should be invited to sit in on the training courses to ensure openness and to enable them to make constructive comments for improvement and to remind the government of its responsibility to ensure that training will have an impact on the daily work practices of officials and in the lives of those in the community they serve.

At the same time, it is important to ensure the impartiality and professionalism of those NGOs involved and when appropriate offer them opportunities to enhance their own skills in this field.

6) Target groups for training and the goals of the course need to be carefully identified.

There can be different approaches and the one adopted will depend on the context in which the training is to be developed – gravity of the violations, the specific country, and other key factors.

Some examples:

- One approach would be to guarantee that only entire units or divisions would be trained, to ensure that each participant takes the training seriously and to avoid the problem of negative peer pressure when the individual trainee returns to his or her unit. Unit training can make follow-up easier and enable unit and commander or head of division performance easier to evaluate and easier to take into account in promotions and transfers.
- Another approach would be to start by only training the trainers (i.e. trainers from military or police academies or law faculty professors), these trainers then participating in the training of the rest of the unit or department. In both cases it is important that human rights training has become or is in the process of becoming a permanent and integrated part of the training curricula for the specific force or branch (supported by the necessary legislative changes).
- A third approach would be to balance training entire units and training a cross-section of officials or trainers. The rationale behind such a mixture would be that when there is a cross-section of trained officials they would reach out for solidarity with others. One possible format under this approach would be to combine national and regional workshops.

Certain specific issues might also need to be targeted during the course to cover particular human rights violations committed by the group being trained.

7) Trainers should have some connection with the target group.

It makes sense to use trainers who have some connection with the target group being trained, for example, when training the police employ trainers with experience within the police force, or when training civil servants invite trainers with direct work experience within the civil service. This will help ensure that the trainers not only command the required respect, but they also understand the difficulties encountered by the trainees in the terrain.

Trainers should be chosen with great care. They must command authority and be impartial. If trainers do not have the necessary pedagogical skills and comparative human rights knowledge, it is questionable whether they should be the preferred choice. The wrong choice of trainers can place into jeopardy the credibility of an entire training program and any confidence building the program may have on restoring public opinion.

The training of trainers from the targeted sectors as well as from relevant NGOs is important so as to ensure that a larger and professional pool of trainers is available. Preliminary work may be necessary to encourage their participation as well as the development of their training skills and human rights knowledge.

8) The teaching methods used should respect the local cultural and religious realities as well as reflect the human rights aims of the training.

Teaching methods need to be adjusted to the particular country, the group being trained and the human rights violations which have occurred or are in danger of occurring in that country. Teaching methods have to be sensitive to cultural and religious practices without sacrificing human rights standards and they need to be accessible to the audience to be effective.

9) The training should be practically oriented and involve participatory learning techniques.

Judges should be asked to decide hypothetical cases at mock trials or appeals, as relevant. Police should be asked to carry out crowd control exercises, mock arrests and interrogation sessions with difficult "subjects" and be asked to react when they see ill-treatment occurring or other violations in a demonstration by fellow students.

Trainers should avoid methods such as when teaching about torture, giving examples of torture techniques used around the world, and then telling students that these methods are wrong. It is preferable to discuss the fact that human rights violations are international, regional and national crimes subject to punishment.

10) The teaching materials should be practically oriented.

The materials have to be made available to participants as far in advance of the training sessions as possible. Each set of materials should include complete texts of the relevant international, regional and national standards (these will vary with the target group) in the appropriate languages. In many countries, however, the majority of the population, including members of the security forces, are illiterate; other materials will have to be developed to ensure that the essence of the principles is imparted.

Where relevant, literacy programs should be a long-range goal for any professional training program, providing a solid framework for any human rights training component.

11) Follow-up must be integrated into the training program from the beginning.

No program should ever be conducted without effective follow-up. Follow-up programs should offer support and when necessary advice to the local trainers and educational/training policy makers, ensuring continuity and high standards.

Possible follow-up techniques include reunions of persons trained, a newsletter about the implementation of training programs (exchange of experiences), activity reports or evaluation reports and contact with participants after training programs to check on progress in implementing what was learned.

12) There must be continuous evaluation of the impact of the program and revision in light of identified shortcomings and new opportunities.

It is important that criteria on which the program is to be evaluated as well as who is to do the evaluation are built in to the program from the start.

Such evaluation must not only be done by the trainers, the trainees and the government unit heads, but by an independent body (such as an NGO or an academic institution) which can carry out an objective evaluation of the program's effectiveness, and provide appropriate recommendations. The implementation of such recommendations also needs to be monitored both by the governmental body in question and by civil society, as well as international agencies.

Each participant should commit himself or herself to taking some practical step to use the training. For example, prosecutors should report what steps they took to investigate each complaint or report of torture or ill-treatment and explain how that was consistent with the training program. This will be crucial in having a concrete impact in improving the human rights situation and taking permanent steps towards the construction of a culture of human rights and development.

The government should assess work related performance to determine whether the recipients are complying with human rights standards and accordingly reward those who adhere to them and sanction those who do not. Human rights training should not be a window-dressing.

Appendix II: Amnesty International's 12-Point Program for the Prevention of Torture by Agents of the State

Torture is a fundamental violation of human rights, condemned by the international community as an offence to human dignity and prohibited in all circumstances under international law.

Yet torture persists, daily and across the globe. Immediate steps are needed to confront torture and other cruel, inhuman or degrading treatment or punishment wherever they occur and to eradicate them totally.

Amnesty International calls on all governments to implement the following 12-Point Program for the Prevention of Torture by Agents of the State. It invites concerned individuals and organizations to ensure that they do so. Amnesty International believes that the implementation of these measures is a positive indication of a government's commitment to end torture and to work for its eradication worldwide.

1) Condemn torture

The highest authorities of every country should demonstrate their total opposition to torture. They should condemn torture unreservedly whenever it occurs. They should make clear to all members of the police, military and other security forces that torture will never be tolerated.

2) Ensure access to prisoners

Torture often takes place while prisoners are held incommunicado – unable to contact people outside who could help them or find out what is happening to them. The practice of incommunicado detention should be ended. Governments should ensure that all prisoners are brought before an independent judicial authority without delay after being taken into custody. Prisoners should have access to relatives, lawyers and doctors without delay and regularly thereafter.

3) No secret detention

In some countries torture takes place in secret locations, often after the victims are made to "disappear". Governments should ensure that prisoners are held only in officially recognized places of detention and that accurate information about their arrest and whereabouts is made available immediately to relatives, lawyers and the courts. Effective judicial remedies should be available to enable relatives and lawyers to find out immediately where a prisoner is held and under what authority and to ensure the prisoner's safety.

4) Provide safeguards during detention and interrogation

All prisoners should be immediately informed of their rights. These include the right to lodge complaints about their treatment and to have a judge rule without delay on the lawfulness of their detention. Judges should investigate any evidence of torture and order release if the detention is unlawful. A lawyer should be present during interrogations. Governments should ensure that conditions of detention conform to international standards for the treatment of prisoners and take into account the needs of members of particularly vulnerable groups. The authorities responsible for detention should be separate from those in charge of interrogation. There should be regular, independent, unannounced and unrestricted visits of inspection to all places of detention.

5) Prohibit torture in law

Governments should adopt laws for the prohibition and prevention of torture incorporating the main elements of the UN Convention against Torture and other Cruel, Inhuman or Degrading Treatment or Punishment (Convention against Torture) and other relevant international standards. All judicial and administrative corporal punishments should be abolished. The prohibition of torture and the essential safeguards for its prevention must not be suspended under any circumstances, including states of war or other public emergency.

6) Investigate

All complaints and reports of torture should be promptly, impartially and effectively investigated by a body independent of the alleged perpetrators. The methods and findings of such investigations should be made public. Officials suspected of committing torture should be suspended from active duty during the investigation. Complainants, witnesses and others at risk should be protected from intimidation and reprisals.

7) Prosecute

Those responsible for torture must be brought to justice. This principle should apply wherever alleged torturers happen to be, whatever their nationality or position, regardless of where the crime was committed and the nationality of the victims, and no matter how much time has elapsed since the commission of the crime. Governments must exercise universal jurisdiction over alleged torturers or extradite them, and cooperate with each other in such criminal proceedings. Trials must be fair. An order from a superior officer must never be accepted as a justification for torture.

8) No use of statements extracted under torture

Governments should ensure that statements and other evidence obtained through torture may not be invoked in any proceedings, except against a person accused of torture.

9) Provide effective training

It should be made clear during the training of all officials involved in the custody, interrogation or medical care of prisoners that torture is a criminal act. Officials should be instructed that they have the right and duty to refuse to obey any order to torture.

10) Provide reparation

Victims of torture and their dependants should be entitled to obtain prompt reparation from the state including restitution, fair and adequate financial compensation and appropriate medical care and rehabilitation.

11) **Ratify international treaties**

All governments should ratify without reservations international treaties containing safeguards against torture, including the UN Convention against Torture with declarations providing for individual and inter-state complaints. Governments should comply with the recommendations of international bodies and experts on the prevention of torture.

12) **Exercise international responsibility**

Governments should use all available channels to intercede with the governments of countries where torture is reported. They should ensure that transfers of training and equipment for military, security or police use do not facilitate torture. Governments must not forcibly return a person to a country where he or she risks being tortured.

This 12-Point Program was adopted by Amnesty International in October 2000 as a program of measures to prevent the torture and ill-treatment of people who are in governmental custody or otherwise in the hands of agents of the state. Amnesty International holds governments to their international obligations to prevent and punish torture, whether committed by agents of the state or by other individuals. Amnesty International also opposes torture by armed political groups.

Endnotes

1. Hooliganism with aggravating circumstances, Article 213, part 2 of the Criminal Code.

2. Article 63 of the Criminal Code lays down the general rule that having "motives of national, racial or religious hatred or enmity" for committing a crime constitute an aggravating circumstance.

3. Prosecutor General Vladimir Ustinov in an interview with the Russian news agency *Interfax*, following reports that a woman had been injured in an explosion while trying to remove an anti-semitic sign from the side of a road, 27 May 2002.

4. The World Conference against Racism, Racial Discrimination, Xenophobia and Related Intolerance was held in August and September 2001 in Durban, South Africa.

5. Prisoners of conscience are people detained solely on account of their political, religious or other conscientiously held beliefs or because of their ethnic origin, sex, colour, language, national or social origin, economic status, birth or other status – who have not used or advocated violence.

6. Amnesty International calls for all prisoners whose cases have a political aspect to be given a prompt and fair trial on recognizably criminal charges, or released. It calls on authorities to ensure that all proceedings are conducted in accordance with international standards of fairness and do not result in the imposition of the death penalty. These include, for example, respect of the presumption of innocence and the rights to a fair hearing before a competent, independent and impartial tribunal; to have adequate time and facilities to prepare a defence; and to appeal to a higher tribunal.

7. AI Index: ACT 40/020/2001 available at www.amnesty.org

8. See www.unhchr.ch/html/racism/Durban.htm

9. Union of Council for Soviet Jews, the organization which has been working actively with Jews in the former Soviet Union since 1970 and produces *Antisemitism, Xenophobia and Religious Persecution in Russia's Regions*, the most comprehensive survey of racism and xenophobia in the former Soviet Union, and recently helped produce a further report, *Nationalism, Xenophobia and Intolerance in Contemporary Russia*, on the subject in collaboration with the Moscow Helsinki Group.

10. *Rehabilitation of the Peoples of Russia: A collection of documents*, Moscow, Insan, 2000.

11. There has been no census in the 13 years since 1989. The first census in the Russian Federation since the demise of the Soviet Union was scheduled for October 2002 with results due to be announced in 2004.

12. Jews were considered a "nationality" by the authorities.

13. See, for example, *Russian Federation/Chechnya: For the Motherland* (AI Index: EUR 46/046/1999) and *The Russian Federation: Denial of justice* (AI Index: EUR 46/027/2002).

14. Sources: Association of African Students at the Russian University of Peoples' Friendship, Moscow.

15. Presumably referring to a police lock-up used for the short-term detention of vagrants and others without recognized identity documents.

16. From a complaint by Usam Vakhaevich Baisaev, sent to the Minister of the Interior of Ingushetia on 16 June 2001, included as Appendix 3 in a report by S.A. Gannushkina, Memorial Human Rights Center, Migration Rights Network entitled *Internally Displaced Persons from Chechnya in the Russian Federation*, Moscow 2002.

17. Article 5(b) of the International Convention on the Elimination of All Forms of Racial Discrimination.

18. Article 14 of the International Convention on the Elimination of All Forms of Racial Discrimination.

19. Communication by the government of the Russian Federation to diplomatic missions in Moscow, January 1992.

20. The former Soviet Union made a declaration under Article 14 of the International Convention on the Elimination of All Forms of Racial Discrimination which entered into force in 1991.

21. The first 11 periodic reports to CERD were submitted by the former Soviet Union. UN Doc. HRI/GEN/1/REV.4. See www.unhchr.ch.tbs

22. UN Doc. CERD/C/304/Add.5, 28 March 1996.

23. CERD General Recommendation XIII on the training of law enforcement officials in the protection of human rights (Forty-second session, 1993) states:

1　*In accordance with article 2, paragraph 1, of the International Convention on the Elimination of All forms of Racial Discrimination, State parties have undertaken that all public authorities and public institutions, national and local, will not engage in any practice of racial discrimination; further, States parties have undertaken to guarantee the rights listed in article 5 of the Convention to everyone without distinction as to race, colour or national or ethnic origin.*

2　*The fulfilment of these obligations very much depends upon national law enforcement officials who exercise police powers, especially the powers of detention or arrest, and upon whether they are properly informed about the obligations their State has entered into under the Convention. Law enforcement officials should receive intensive training to ensure that in the performance of their duties they respect as well as protect human dignity and maintain and uphold the human rights of all persons without distinction as to race, colour or national or ethnic origin.*

3　*In the implementation of article 7 of the Convention, the Committee calls upon States parties to review and improve the training of law enforcement officials so that the standards of the Convention as well as the Code of Conduct for Law Enforcement Officials (1979) are fully implemented. They should also include respective information thereupon in their periodic reports.*

24. UN Doc. CERD/C/299/Add.15.

25. UN Doc. CERD/C /304/Add. 43, 30 March 1998.

26. Article 282 makes it a criminal offence to engage in deliberate acts intended to stir up national, racial or religious hatred or discord, to detract from national honour or dignity, to promote the idea of exclusiveness of the inferiority of citizens because of their religious beliefs, nationality or race, or directly or indirectly to restrict the rights of or establish privileges for citizens because of their race, nationality, or attitude to religion.

Article 63 lays down the general rule that having "motives of national, racial or religious hatred or enmity" for committing a crime is an aggravating circumstance.

27. During that period three reports, the 15th, 16th and 17th, should have been submitted in 1998, 2000 and 2002 respectively.

28. *East African Asians v the United Kingdom*, 14 December 1973, Appl. Nos. 4403/70 et al, reproduced in 3 European Human Rights Reports 76.

29. Protocol No. 12 to the Convention for the Protection of Human Rights and Fundamental Freedoms, http://conventions.coe.int/treaty/EN/cadreprincipal.htm.

30. Protocol No. 12 will come into force three months after 10 states have ratified it. At the time of writing, 29 of the 44 Council of Europe member states had signed Protocol No. 12; two of these had also ratified it.

31. Article 1 of the European Convention for the Prevention of Torture and Inhuman or Degrading Treatment or Punishment.

32. The Russian Federation has allowed publication of the preliminary observations of the CPT delegation which travelled to the North Caucasus region in late February 2000.

33. CPT Doc. CPT/inf(2001)15, available on the CPT's website at www.cpt.coe.int

34. http://www.coe.int/T/E/human_rights/Ecri

35. Second report on the Russian Federation, ECRI, CRI (2001) 41.

36. Interview with the radio station *Ekho Moskvy*, 10 December 2001.

37. *Working against Racism in Russia: Perspective of Russian NGOs*, published by the NGO Network Against Racism and The Center for the Development of Democracy and Human Rights, August 2001.

38. See the European Commission against Racism and Intolerance's Second Report on the Russian Federation, adopted on 16 March 2001, Doc. CRI(2001)41, paras 76, 78 and 80; Resolution 1277 of the Parliamentary Assembly of the Council of Europe, adopted in April 2002; and Concluding Observations of the Committee on the Rights of the Child: Russian Federation, 10 November 1999, UN Doc. CRC/C/15/Add.110, paras 51 and 52.

39. Internally Displaced Persons from Chechnya in the Russian Federation, Svetlana Gannushkina, Memorial Human Rights Center Migration Rights Network, Moscow.

40. Said-Emin (last name withheld) was interviewed by an Amnesty International delegate in October 2001 and February 2002.

41. See also *Russian Federation/Chechnya: For the Motherland* (AI Index: EUR 46/046/1999).

42. Article 228 (1) of the Criminal Code.

43. Issue No. 26 (1027).

44. Article 228, part 4 and Article 222 of the Criminal Code of the Russian Federation respectively.

45. Letter from Inna Aylamazyan of 9 February 2001 to a senior officer at a local police station.

46. For further details see *Russian Federation/Chechnya: For the Motherland* (AI Index: EUR 46/046/1999).

47. Extract from a letter from Inna Aylamazyan to the Deputy Chair of the Committee on CIS Affairs, state *Duma* Deputy Igrunov, and to the Ambassador of the Republic of Tajikistan to the Russian Federation.

48. See *The Russian Federation: Denial of Justice* (AI Index: EUR 46/027/2002), pp. 34 to 37.

49. This information on these cases is based on data and material given to Amnesty International by the defence lawyer, Inna Ailamazian, in various conversations during 2002; also correspondence with Olga Cherepova of Memorial, Inna Aylamazian's letter to state *Duma* Deputy Igrunov and the Ambassador of Tajikistan to the Russian Federation, R.Z. Mirzoev, in May 2001, and from Deputy Igrunov to the General Prosecutor around the same time.

50. Human Rights Committee, General Comment 20, 1992, available on www.unhchr.ch/tbs/doc.nsf

51. *A v United Kingdom*, judgment of the European Court of Human Rights, 28 September 1998. http://hudoc.echr.coe.int/hudoc.

52. Article 2(1)(d) and Article 5(b).

53. The standard of due diligence was applied by the Inter-American Court of Human Rights in its judgment in 1988 on the Velásquez-Rodríguez case: "An illegal act which violates human rights and which is initially not directly imputable to the State (for example, because it is an act of a private person or because the person responsible has not been identified) can lead to international responsibility of the State, not because of the act itself but because of the lack of due diligence to prevent the violation or to respond to it as required by the Convention." This standard has been incorporated into international instruments and elaborated on by human rights experts and mechanisms of the UN as well as by national courts.

54. The group surveyed was made up of 125 men and 55 women. In general the African population in Moscow is disproportionately male because more men are likely to be sent to the Russian Federation as students.

55. Adefers Dessu was interviewed by Amnesty International representatives in November 2001 and June 2002.

56. For further information on the Meskhetians, see *Russian Experience of Ethnic Discrimination: Meskhetians in Krasnodar Region*, Alexander G. Osipov, Memorial Human Rights Center, Moscow, 2000.

57. Population estimates from Alexander Osipov.

58. Article 13(1) of the 1991 Law On Citizenship did not define "permanent residence" as "permanent registration".

59. The law On Measures to Reinforce State Control over Migration and on Administrative Eviction of Persons Illegally in Krasnodar Territory (No. 1381-P of 27 March 2002) and the law On Temporary and Permanent Residence in Krasnodar Territory (No. 460 of 11 April 2002).

60. No. 1363-P.

61. There are many definitions of the term "Cossack". For example, the Cossacks were defined as an ethnic group in the 1991 Russian Soviet Federative Socialist Republic Law on the Rehabilitation of Repressed Peoples. There are also Cossack associations which have a semi-official status governed by presidential decree. They also act as an auxiliary police force whose activities are governed by agreements with local representatives of the Ministry of the Interior.

62. Expert comments on the Law of Krasnodar Territory of 1 April 2002, No. 460-KZ "On temporary and permanent residence in Krasnodar Territory" at the request of Russian NGO Memorial, by Mara Fedorovna Poliakova of the NGO Independent Council of Legal Experts, dated 8 May 2002. See www.hro.org

63. See, for example, Constitutional Court decisions of April 1995, April 1996, July 1997 and February 1998.

64. Article 1 of the Law of the Krasnodar Territory of 1 April 2002.

65. Article 4 of the Law of the Krasnodar Territory of 1 April 2002.

66. Articles 13 and 14 of the Law of the Krasnodar Territory of 1 April 2002.

67. Article 8 of the Law of the Krasnodar Territory of 1 April 2002.

68. Articles 18 and 19 of the Law of the Krasnodar Territory of 1 April 2002.

69. In mid-2001 the authorities issued an instruction giving effect to Article 12 of the Law on Refugees. Under this article people can receive temporary humanitarian asylum, on a case by case basis, not under the strict refugee definition. The terms last for a year at a time. There are, however, problems with attempts by the authorities to apply limitations, such as denying access to the determination procedure on grounds of illegal entry, "safe third country" and failure to apply within 24 hours, limitations that are also applied to those seeking refugee status.

70. Based on an interview with Brice Ewalaka-Koumou and his lawyer by an Amnesty International delegate, St Petersburg, May 2002.

71. The CIS comprises 12 states, all from the former Soviet Union – Armenia, Azerbaijan, Belarus, Georgia, Kazakstan, Kyrgyzstan, Moldova, Russia, Tajikistan, Turkmenistan, Ukraine and Uzbekistan. Estonia, Latvia and Lithuania opted not to join the CIS.

72. Meeting with Samuel Davies in Moscow, 20 May 2002. Information on Severny was also obtained from people who had visited men imprisoned there and from UNHCR monitoring.

73. 2002 law on the Legal Situation of Foreign Citizens in the Russian Federation, Articles 33 and 34.

74. Conclusion 44(b) of the UNHCR's Programme (EXCOM).

75. Further guidance can be found in the 1999 UNHCR Guidelines on Applicable Criteria and Standards relating to the Detention of Asylum-Seekers.

76. Ministry of the Interior website, 27 July 2002.

77. Meeting with staff at the Moscow Office of the UNHCR, March 2002.

78. Meeting with staff at the Moscow Office of the UNHCR, March 2002.

79. For more information see UNHCR press release of 5 April 2001.

80. According to estimates of the Moscow Office of the UNHCR, 3,000 undocumented people were detected at Sheremetevo II over the two years from 2000 to 2002.

81. Letter of 3 May 2002.

82. *Background on the situation in the Russian Federation in the context of the return of asylum-seekers*, UNHCR Geneva, October 2000.

83. General Recommendation XIII on the training of law enforcement officials in the protection of human rights (Forty-second session, 1993) CERD. See endnote 23 above and www.unhchr.ch/tbs/doc.nsf